W0080906

Can India survive more Modi?

Nine years into his leadership the world has remained silent on Modi's failed democracy. It's time to turn up the temperature before it's too late, writes **JEMIMAH STEINFELD**

WE AT INDEX have been keeping an eye on India under Narendra Modi ever since he was elected to the office of prime minister in 2014. We have written on a now rescinded law to make standing for the national anthem mandatory in cinemas, for example, and written on women put online for "auction" and on Muslim butchers too afraid to advertise beef.

It was not until a tip-off came in November though that we took a much closer look. We were told about a long-time TV presenter who was becoming a lone critical voice. They feared for their job. Did we want to be put in touch? We said yes, only they were too scared to talk on the record. Then they lost their job and didn't want to talk at all.

This whiff of a story was the spark that turned into a flame and from it our special report. We ascertained that on every key marker of a democracy Modi's India fails. The press, once vibrant, is being strangled; the judiciary is no longer independent; laws have been amended to throw protesters in jail; opposition figures are harassed; minorities live in fear. Statues of Modi go up, ancient mosques come down. A hyper form of ethno-nationalism that we'd more associate with interwar Europe is the doctrine of the land. There is no room for tolerance.

This matters in general and it particularly matters in India, which is set to shortly overtake China as the world's most populous nation and which will head to the polls next year. Why is the world largely silent? Sure, Modi's name will appear on a list with the other so-called "strong men" of today, but the red carpet is rolled out. No one talks about sanctions. Salil Tripathi has a guess in his impassioned essay on India's "flawed" democratic experiment, in which he discusses Modi's long-term goal of a unitary state with a singular faith. A cast of other excellent journalists then take us through the challenges as they live them on the ground, from talking honestly about sex when assault is rife to New Delhi being the most surveilled city in the world.

Perhaps the BBC documentary on Modi – both its content and India's censorial response to it – has been a wake-up call. We hope this report moves the dial even further.

Elsewhere in the magazine we publish an essay from Nariman Dzhelyal, who is the leader of the Crimean Tatars, written from his prison cell. Celebrated Ukrainian writer Andrey Kurkov introduces Dzhelyal and explains why he is such a formidable character. The academic and author Kerry Brown wades into the contentious issue of whether we should ban Confucius Institutes, while Jo-Ann Mort talks about the inventive tactics used by US organisations to fight abortion bans. Finally, Martin Bright reminds us of those Afghan journalists still living under Taliban rule. It's easy for the world to move on to the next disaster, the next big story and that is why Index exists – to not forget. ✖

Jemimah Steinfeld is Index editor-in-chief

52(01):1/1|DOI:10.1177/03064220231165359

A virtual assault

Mark Frary introduces our cover artist

The Big Fat Bao is an illustrator whose work focuses on the intersection of caste, gender and Indian visual design. Their research highlights the casteist roots of Indian design, while their illustrations challenge Hinduism/ Brahmanism. Bao's posts on Instagram have been repeatedly taken down and their account "severely shadowbanned". The cover depicts how fascism in India has taken control of social media apps, torn down the values of peace and democracy by attacking caste minorities, denied access to education to Muslim students by banning them from wearing the hijab in academicl institutions and using JCB machines to demolish the houses of religious and caste minorities.

CONTENTS

INDEXONCENSORSHIP.ORG

CREDIT: The Big Fat Bao

The Index

52(01):4/12|DOI:10.1177/03064220231165360

A round-up of
events in the
world of free
expression
from Index's
unparalleled
network of
writers and
activists

Edited by
MARK FRARY

PICTURED: Prison officers stand guard at a newly inaugurated "Terrorist Confinement Centre" with capacity for 40,000 inmates in El Salvador. The government declared a state of emergency over rising gang violence in March 2022 but many believe the prison serves a double purpose - to lock up government critics too

The Index

ELECTION WATCH

FRANCIS CLARKE looks at what is happening at the poll booths of the world

LEFT TO RIGHT: (Turkey) Recep Tayyip Erdogan; (Cambodia) Hun Sen; (Zimbabwe) Nelson Chamisa

1. Turkey

MAY 2023

At the end of January, an alliance of opposition parties in Turkey vowed to reduce presidential powers if it wins the presidential and parliamentary elections in May. The alliance is concerned about measures implemented by Recep Tayyip Erdogan and his party that it feels is taking Turkey down an authoritarian route, including the abolition of the prime minister role (giving increased powers to the president), control over large parts of the media, as well as the crackdown on dissent after a failed coup in 2016. The deadly earthquakes that struck southern Turkey and northern Syria on 6 February, killing over 55,000 people, meant that choosing a candidate was postponed. The government has faced heavy criticism regarding construction firms that were allowed to bypass safety regulations, and there is the belief that Erdogan will struggle to shake off the crisis when it comes to the court of public opinion. While Erdogan has tried to delay the elections, it would have been deemed unconstitutional to move them beyond June.

2. Cambodia

JULY 2023

Ahead of the July general election, it has been a rough time for the Candlelight Party, now Cambodia's second largest political party. Incidents have included the arrest of its vice president, Thach Setha, for using several bounced cheques, and a defamation lawsuit against one of its advisors, Kong Korm, for comments about the seizure of his property, which the ruling Cambodian People's Party said had "malicious intent" and aimed to cause social unrest. The Candlelight Party became the main opposition party after splitting from the Cambodia National Rescue Party, which was forcibly dissolved by the government in 2017 on the unfounded charge of plotting a coup. On 9 February Prime Minister Hun Sen gave the independent Cambodian news outlet VOD 72 hours to retract allegations about his son Hun Manet, seen to be a future party leader, threatening to revoke its licence if it failed to do so. A report published by the UN Human Rights Office in August stated that journalists in Cambodia are increasingly subjected to various forms of harassment, pressure and violence.

3. Zimbabwe

JULY/AUGUST 2023

Nelson Chamisa, the leader of Zimbabwe's main opposition party, has called on the international community to "keep their eyes on" the southern African country this year, as he warned of violence and repression by the ruling Zanu-PF party in the lead up to national elections. Chamisa, president of the Citizens Coalition for Change, gave the prediction shortly after a gathering of CCC activists in a private residence in the Budiriro township, about 10 miles from the capital Harare, was raided and dozens were detained, with 25 people subsequently appearing in court. Chamisa will be taking on Emmerson Mnangagwa, who became Zimbabwe's president in 2017 following the decades-long rule of Robert Mugabe. He cemented his position by winning the 2018 national election. The Zimbabwe Peace Project, a non-governmental organisation, recorded 263 and 209 reports of assault, threat or intimidation incidents across Zimbabwe in November and December last year respectively. The ZPP claims Zanu-PF was responsible for about 45% of incidents. ✖

UK'S POSITION ON NEW FREEDOM RANKING RAISES EYEBROWS

The country has been ranked only "partially open" in the new Index Index

A MAJOR NEW global ranking produced by Index on Censorship that tracks the state of free expression globally has seen the UK ranked as only "partially open" in every key area measured. In the overall rankings, the UK fell below countries including Australia, Israel, Costa Rica, Chile, Jamaica and Japan. European neighbours such as Austria, Belgium, France, Germany and Denmark also all rank higher than the UK.

The Index Index (**indexoncensorship.org/indexindex**), developed in partnership with experts in machine learning and journalism at Liverpool John Moores University, uses innovative machine learning techniques to map the free expression landscape across the globe, giving a country-by-country view of the state of free expression across academic, digital and media freedoms.

Key findings include:

- The countries with the highest ranking ("open") on the overall Index are clustered around western Europe and Australasia – Australia, Austria, Belgium, Costa Rica, Denmark, Estonia, Finland, Germany, Ireland, Latvia, Lithuania, Netherlands, New Zealand, Norway, Portugal, Sweden and Switzerland.
- The UK and USA join countries such as Botswana, Czechia, Greece, Moldova, Panama, Romania, South Africa and Tunisia ranked as "partially open".
- The poorest performing countries across all metrics, ranked as "closed", are Bahrain, Belarus, Myanmar, China, Cuba, Equatorial Guinea, Eritrea, Eswatini, Laos, Nicaragua, North Korea, Saudi Arabia, South Sudan, Syria, Turkmenistan, United Arab Emirates and Yemen.
- Countries such as China, Russia and Saudi Arabia performed poorly in the Index Index but are embedded in key international mechanisms including G20 and the UN Security Council.

Ruth Anderson, Index on Censorship CEO, said: "The findings of the pilot project are illuminating, surprising and concerning in equal measure. The United Kingdom ranking may well raise some eyebrows, though is not entirely unexpected. Index on Censorship's recent work on issues as diverse as Chinese Communist Party influence in the art world through to the chilling effect of the UK government's Online Safety Bill all point to backward steps for a country that has long viewed itself as a bastion of freedom of expression." ✖

The UK fell below Costa Rica, Chile and Jamaica

Free speech in numbers

5
Years in prison faced by Yemeni fashion model Intisar Abdulrahman Al-Hammadi after she was convicted of "prostitution and drug use" by a court that lacks the minimum international standards for fair trial and legal procedures, according to the Gulf Center for Human Rights. She denies the charges.

1 BILLION
The projected audience for the 2023 Women's World Cup, which FIFA has announced will now not be sponsored by Visit Saudi.

77
The number of countries that have restricted the internet since 2015 according to Netblocks. The latest country on the list is Suriname where police have responded to protests over austerity measures with tear gas and rubber bullets.

10
Number of years sentence given to Burundian journalist Floriane Irangabiye on charges of "undermining the integrity of the national territory" after she interviewed a human rights defender and a journalist, both of whom criticised Burundi's human rights record.

5 trillion
The number of cryptocurrency tokens behind TruthGPT, a proposed "ChatGPT alternative that…is not subject to censorship, manipulation, or any other form of bias".

The Index

PEOPLE WATCH

FRANCIS CLARKE highlights the stories of human rights defenders under attack

Jennifer Awingan-Taggaoa

PHILIPPINES

Jennifer Awingan-Taggaoa is a researcher at Cordillera Peoples Alliance, a group of organisations committed to indigenous and human rights. Taggaoa was arrested, then released on bail, on 7 February along with six other human rights defenders. All were charged with an attack by the New People's Army on Philippine army soldiers in Gacab, causing two deaths. During a hearing, affidavits of surviving soldiers did not identify Awingan-Taggaoa and the defendants as assailants. All were charged as members of the Communist Party of the Philippines.

Raghunath Kha

BANGLADESH

On 29 January, journalist and human rights defender Raghunath Kha was released on bail from Sathkira District Jail in Bangladesh, after being arrested by plain-clothed police on 23 January following a land dispute in Khalishakhali he was reporting on. The land, awarded to underprivileged communities, was being forcibly occupied by land grabbers. It is reported that Kha appeared in a beaten-up state in court the next day, charged with an attempted bomb blast in coordination with landless people. Despite no evidence, this case continues to be investigated.

Jassim Al-Asadi

IRAQ

The environmentalist and human rights defender Jassim Al-Asadi was kidnapped by an unknown armed group on 1 February. An expert on environmental issues, Al-Asadi was travelling to Baghdad to meet the minister of water resources to assist with a plan to irrigate agricultural lands. He was handcuffed and forced into a vehicle; his family believe it is linked to the role of armed groups in environmental abuses and the oil sector. Al-Asadi was outspoken on Iraq's marshlands' conditions, and environmental human rights defenders reportedly face threats and intimidation in the country.

Mohammed Al-Qahtani

SAUDI ARABIA

Mohammed Al-Qahtani, imprisoned since 2013, was due to be released in November 2022 but his whereabouts remain unknown. A human rights defender and economics professor, Al-Qahtani was sentenced in Riyadh to 10 years' imprisonment for setting up the unlicensed Association for Civil and Political Rights in Saudi Arabia. His family have had no contact from him since 23 October 2022. Al-Qahtani's wife's complaints that he was repeatedly assaulted by inmates suffering from mental illnesses during his term may be one of the reasons for his targeting.

Ink spot

This cartoon by Fadi Abou Hassan is a comment on the Orwellian situation emerging in Tunisia where President Kais Saied, elected in 2019, has detained a number of opposition figures, including a politician, a prominent businessman, two judges and a former diplomat, and Noureddine Boutar, the head of the independent radio station Mosaïque FM, which has been critical of the president. Saied says he wants to "save the north African nation from chaos".

In 2021, Saied sacked the prime minister, suspended parliament and pushed through a constitution enshrining his one-man rule.

Hassan, known as FadiToOn, is a widely published and award-winning Palestinian freelance cartoonist. He lived as a refugee in Syria until the uprising in 2011, and is known for his many cartoons commenting on the everyday life and political events in Syria and the Middle East in general.

World In Focus: Nagorno-Karabakh region

Azerbaijan and Armenia met for talks at the Munich Security Conference in February, as conflict escalated in the Nagorno-Karabakh region despite agreement to a Russia-brokered truce

1 Mount Mets Ishkhanasar

A video posted on social media in early October 2022 showed the execution of Armenian prisoners of war, reportedly by Azerbaijani forces during fighting between the countries. The killings took place in September 2022, during one of several breakdowns of the 2020 Russia-brokered truce that ended hostilities in the unresolved conflict. At least seven Armenian POWs are thought to have died, in what the advocacy group Human Rights Watch called a "war crime for which there needs to be accountability". The French newspaper Libération said the video was filmed between Mount Mets Ishkhanasar and Small Ishkhanasar Mountain, along Armenia's southeastern border with Azerbaijan.

Azerbaijan is a party to the International Covenant on Civil and Political Rights and the European Convention on Human Rights, both of which strictly forbid extrajudicial killings.

2 The Lachin Corridor

The Russian-backed ceasefire signed in 2020 guaranteed safe passage for civilians and provisions along the Lachin Corridor, which is the only transport link between Nagorno-Karabakh and Armenia. Food and medical supplies are failing to reach the approximately 120,000-strong Armenian population of the region after the road was blockaded by Azerbaijani environmental protesters, believed to be backed by the country's authorities. Gas supplies were also cut off, with the Azerbaijan state-owned gas firm Azeriqaz blaming bad weather, with supplies reinstated in December 2022.

Azerbaijani officials said that Armenian allegations of a humanitarian blockade of the corridor was "fake news" and the free movement of humanitarian cargo was

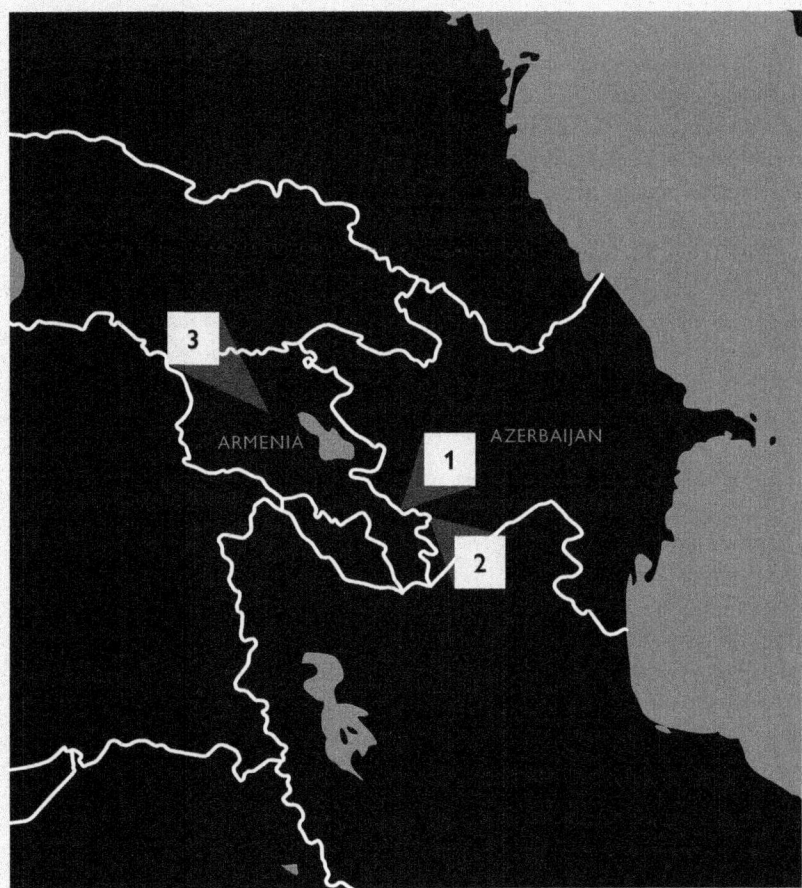

ensured, while Amnesty International has described the situation as a humanitarian crisis, saying "Azerbaijan fails its human rights obligations by taking no action to lift the blockade."

3 Armenia

Experts and human rights activists say Armenian authorities could be using the threat of renewed hostilities with Azerbaijan to seize emergency wartime powers. Due to renewed conflict in the Nagorno-Karabakh region, there are fears that under martial law, the government

is using the legal ability to censor online content, block media outlets and even curb internet access. The potential of the bill, drawn up by the Justice Ministry in December 2022, would also allow the shutdown of internet access altogether.

Freedom House classed the internet in Armenia as "free", with a score of 74 out of 100 in its 2022 Freedom on the Net report. This was an improvement on the 2021 report, when restrictions on the free flow of information in Armenia were imposed during conflict with Azerbaijani forces in the Nagorno-Karabakh region.

The Index

TECH WATCH

TIKTOK AND YOU DON'T STOP

US law-makers want to ban the controversial app. This is not the answer says **MARK FRARY**

US REPUBLICAN SENATOR Josh Hawley and Congressman Ken Buck recently introduced the No TikTok on Government Devices Act, which would mean the popular video-sharing platform would be completely banned in the USA. The politicians proposing the new act are worried about TikTok because of its ownership and reach.

Announcing the proposed legislation, Buck said in a statement: "TikTok is a clear threat to our privacy and national security. Not only is TikTok directly associated with the Chinese Communist Party (CCP), but it has been used to spy on Americans and gain an alarming level of access to users' phones."

Buck's comments on TikTok's links with the CCP are not without substance. TikTok was launched in 2016 by the Chinese company ByteDance. Shou Zi Chew, TikTok's Singapore-born CEO (who studied at University College London and Harvard), says the Chinese state owns 1% of Beijing Douyin Information Service Limited, a subsidiary of ByteDance. He says the company was required to sell the stake to the government so that it could obtain a licence for its China-based operations.

Reuters reported that ByteDance censored anti-China content in Indonesia

Shou argues that the CCP does not have any control over TikTok. It is also worth noting that ByteDance's investors also include US companies such as General Atlantic and KKR.

In September 2022, US senators grilled TikTok chief operating officer Vanessa Pappas in a hearing about TikTok's ties to the CCP. Pappas said that no person who "makes a strategic decision" at TikTok is a CCP member but could not say whether any of its employees were. She added that the company has not been asked for US user data by the CCP and would not hand over any even if asked.

Some say there is reason to think this would not be the case. In 2020, for example, Reuters reported that ByteDance had censored anti-China content in Indonesia.

The proposed new legislation would expand on a ban on the app on government devices introduced as part of the 2022 year-end omnibus spending bill, also led by Senator Hawley. The US House of Representatives chief administrative officer Catherine Szpindor had previously issued a cyber advisory saying it did not recommend the download or use of the TikTok application as it had been identified as "high risk to users due to its lack of transparency in how it protects customer data".

The new bill faces a number of challenges, not least that it seems to fly in the face of the First Amendment, which says that "Congress shall make no law...abridging the freedom of speech".

However, ever since the Bill of Rights was introduced, there have been exceptions to this in the event of war or other threats to national security. Just seven years after the First Amendment was introduced, Congress adopted the Sedition Act, which made it a crime for US citizens to "print, utter, or publish... any false, scandalous, and malicious writing" about the government.

There are precedents for government bans on TikTok. On 29 June 2020, the Indian government banned the platform along with 58 other apps including WeChat and Weibo, which "harm India's sovereignty as well as the privacy of [its] citizens". At the time of the ban's announcement, the platform had at least 200 million users in the country. It remains banned today. The focus has now moved to the USA where the platform has the highest number of users.

What may be surprising to some is that TikTok is also blocked in China. There people are allowed to access Douyin, also operated by ByteDance and offering similar functionality. In September 2021, it launched Youth Mode, a version of the app for under 14s that only allows 40 minutes of daily usage and that shuts off after 10pm. Under 18s must have parental consent to use the app, which also promotes additional "educational" content to children.

TikTok argues that it is working hard to address the US government's concerns. In June 2022, it said it had been working on something called Project Texas for more than a year. This "multi-pronged initiative" is intended to achieve "compliance with a final

agreement with the US Government that will fully safeguard user data and US national security interests".

Project Texas involves US companies, including IT services company Oracle and consulting firm Booz Allen. TikTok says that 100% of US user data is now stored by default in the Oracle cloud environment and is working to delete US users' data from any other cloud or backup server located elsewhere.

TikTok now has more than one billion active users. Things that appear on it travel around the world and are amplified in an instant and this has not gone unnoticed by social activists. In the protests following the death of Jina ("Mahsa") Amini at the hands of Iran's morality police last September, protesters used TikTok to share videos of the protests, mislabelling them to get around the country's strict internet censorship. The song Baraye by Iranian singer-songwriter Shervin Hajipour, whose lyrics are based on a series of Farsi tweets that details Iranians' reasons for

protesting, has been used as the audio backdrop for many of these videos. Black activists have also used TikTok to highlight racial inequality in the Black Lives Matter protests.

Countries such as Indonesia, Brazil, Russia, Mexico and Turkey, where freedom of expression is under pressure, are also in the top 10 countries in terms of user numbers for TikTok.

Despite what Hawley and Buck think, a ban on TikTok is not the answer. Countries like the USA, where freedom of expression is valued, should recognise that platforms such as TikTok

 The Indian government banned the platform along with 58 other apps

ABOVE: An anti-TikTok demonstration takes place in Kolkata after skirmishes on the India-China border

give people a voice. Banning TikTok will silence many of those voices.

That said, there is nothing to stop regulators both in the USA and elsewhere introducing new measures, or expanding existing ones such as the EU's GDPR rules, to ensure that data privacy is respected.

Monitoring and moderating the content people see on the platform will be harder. The machine-learning algorithm that chooses the videos people are offered in their feeds is particularly effective, driving its "addictive" nature and hence the Chinese ban for under 14s. Even though TikTok has developed this algorithm, the way it picks specific content is largely opaque. This is as much a question for ethicists as it is for big tech companies and politicians. ✖

Mark Frary is associate editor at Index

The Index

MY INSPIRATION

WALKING TALL WITH A BROKEN BACK

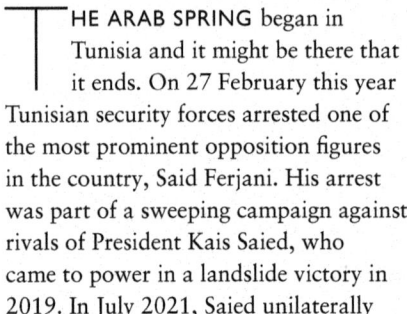

Said Ferjani has campaigned for decades for freedoms in Tunisia. For this he has been jailed - twice

THE ARAB SPRING began in Tunisia and it might be there that it ends. On 27 February this year Tunisian security forces arrested one of the most prominent opposition figures in the country, Said Ferjani. His arrest was part of a sweeping campaign against rivals of President Kais Saied, who came to power in a landslide victory in 2019. In July 2021, Saied unilaterally

PICTURED: Said Ferjani at an Oxford Union debate about what the Arab Spring achieved

suspended parliament and dissolved the government in what many have labelled a "constitutional coup". Since then Saied has lost popularity and has responded by rounding up opposition figures, with Ferjani being one.

Ferjani was born in 1954 in Kairouan, a sacred city in northern Tunisia. He is a long-time member of the Ennahda Party, a political party governed by a dual commitment to moderate Islam and to democracy and pluralism. Ferjani was previously

arrested by the late dictator Zine El Abedine Ben Ali in 1987, when the Ennahda Party was outlawed, and spent 18 months in prison. He later fled to the UK to seek asylum on a passport he had borrowed from a friend. After the popular revolution that ousted Ben Ali from power in 2011, Ferjani returned to Tunisia and was elected as an MP for Ennahda, serving as a party adviser.

His daughter, Kaouther Ferjani, shares her memory of growing up with him, his steely spirit and why he wouldn't do his life differently.

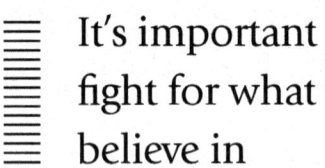

It's important to fight for what you believe in

I WAS THREE years old the first time my father was made a prisoner of conscience. It was 1987 under the Ben Ali regime, and like the dictator before him, he was cracking down on those who opposed him. My father was one of them.

When I would visit him in prison with my mother, he was always smiling despite the torture he endured. Even when he looked tired at times, he was never defeated - my father's spirit was always there.

When he was temporarily released, he was in a wheelchair as his back was broken from torture. He knew he had to leave before they took him again, so he trained himself to walk without showing any sign of pain long enough to get through airport security. And it worked. He came to the UK in 1989 and until Tunisia's revolution in 2011, my father never stopped advocating for

democracy and human rights in Tunisia.

He is now 68 and in prison again without charge and without evidence, for opposing yet another dictator. Every time I find myself giving into the pain of this injustice and imagining what indignities he must be facing at his age, I remind myself of his strength and resilience. Before his impending imprisonment, he told me he still chooses this life and that it's important to fight for what you believe in, especially when others need you to. He's been on hunger strike for the last nine days, his health is deteriorating, but he refuses to back down.

My father embodies bravery and conviction. He is not only my inspiration; he is my motivation to keep fighting on his behalf for all those unjustly imprisoned. ✖

By Kaouther Ferjani

CREDIT: Pierre Crom/Gett

FEATURES

"The main purpose of this crime - the creation of a
new big lie about the small indigenous people of
Crimea - is the repression of the peninsula itself"

Cultural amnesia in Cairo

Artists are under attack in the Egyptian capital, where the government has scrubbed all signs of the revolution from the streets. **NICK HILDEN** reports

AT THE CENTRE of Cairo is Tahrir Square, which in 2011 was the focal point for Egypt's revolution that ended the 30-year reign of president Hosni Mubarak. Two years later, Egyptians took to the streets again, this time to depose his successor, Mohamed Morsi, in what evolved into a military coup. Abdel Fattah el-Sisi has held power ever since.

Today, when you visit Tahrir, the once grassy circle at its centre has been replaced by a looming Pharaonic monument. There are words printed on it, but you cannot read them because a round-the-clock security force aggressively prevents you from approaching. This is, in a way, the perfect metaphor for the present situation in Egypt. A revolutionary history enshrouded. Words that cannot be read. The manifest expression of state control.

It is worth noting that "*tahrir*" is Arabic for "liberation", which is ironically absent from the square.

"Did you notice how many cameras there are?" asked a prominent Egyptian artist I spoke to during a recent visit to Cairo who, for safety reasons, will be referred to as "Salma". I had just mentioned an abundance of new planters and other obstacles that had been installed throughout the square – obvious attempts to make mass congregation impossible.

"Every building has two or three cameras," she said. "They completely eradicated any trace of the revolution. They aggressively removed all graffiti. They removed all the police booths – the historic ones – because we used to spray-paint them. Those are gone."

Graffiti, which was once a common expression of social change in Egypt, is conspicuously absent from the walls of downtown Cairo. Not only has the revolutionary street art been covered up but those who would wield paint to create it receive harsh punishments – as do many other politically vocal artists and figures in Egypt which, according to human rights groups, currently holds as

many as 65,000 political prisoners in jail.

Sentences can be long and uncertain "depending on the medium and the kind of insult", Salma explained. "If

> Breaking the law can be translated to any form they want. They shift it based on their mood

ABOVE: A graffitied wall blocks access to the Ministry of the Interior near Cairo's Tahrir Square, during a time of mass protests in 2012

it's political graffiti and it's critical, it's up to four years in jail and a fine. And the offences are very loose: insulting religion, breaking the law...I mean, breaking the law can be translated to any form they want. They shift it based on their mood."

For an example of these "loose" punishments, take the story of poet Galal el-Behairy. Back during the first revolution of 2011, musician Ramy Essam penned a song called Irhal ("Leave") that became regarded as the anthem of the protests. More than half a decade later, he collaborated with el-Behairy on a song criticising Sisi entitled Balaha, which they released via a music video that bore the names of its production team. The crackdown was swift. El-Behairy, who wrote the lyrics, was imprisoned for the "crimes" of blasphemy, insulting the military, contempt of religion, dissemination of false news and a range of other trumped-up charges. Essam was forced to flee into exile. And the video's director, Shady Habash, was arrested and died in prison under dubious circumstances.

Avant Garde Lawyers, an organisation which provides legal aid to artists under attack around the world, came to el-Behairy's defence and managed to argue what began as a potential life sentence down to three years. But at the conclusion of his sentence, when his family went to retrieve him from prison, they were told that he had disappeared. Eventually they learned that he had been moved to another prison, where he remains to this day, regardless of his now long-finished sentence.

El-Behairy had broken the number-one rule for artists under the regime which, according to Salma, is: "Don't criticise the president. Say nothing about their philosophy and their outlook, which is 'building a better future for all of us' – from their point of view."

All of this is part of the government's counter-revolutionary efforts.

"They're spending a lot of money on that," Salma said. "They are literally erasing all traces of the revolution. We have to keep the story because they are systematically erasing everything aggressively. It's an agenda. Collective amnesia."

Artists who attempt to tell the story or push back against the government agenda receive a harsh rebuke. Actors Amr Waked and Khaled Abol Naga were both banned from Egypt and now live in exile in the USA for criticising Sisi's recent changes to the constitution, which will allow him to remain in office

They are literally erasing all traces of the revolution

until 2034. And for political artists in the country, the prospect of prison poses a very real danger.

The Egyptian state press centre did not respond to questions about the imprisoned and exiled artists.

Before leaving the country, I attended the Art Cairo event, at which a number of artists spoke on the topic of artistic censorship – among them, Egyptian-Lebanese artist Lara Baladi.

According to Baladi, the struggle is "to navigate the censorship in a way that we are pushing the boundaries but we are not falling off the cliff".

She added: "We have to go all the way and push all that we can, but also protect ourselves and make sure that we are still able to express ourselves. That's a very fine line. It's almost like walking on a thread between two mountains. It's a constant challenge. Censorship and challenge are exactly why we are artists, in a way. It's a very important aspect of being creative."

Her advice to artists creating under oppression is to understand the environment and how to navigate it so they can do their work.

"If you confront something that is prohibited, you're bound to end up in jail or be shut down, or even exiled," she said. "It's a matter of being subtle about what we do so that we can actually continue to express ourselves.

"It's very difficult to be censored – it's not constructive – because, ultimately, what this means is that nobody sees you. So it's more important to try to say things without being provocative than to be provocative and end up in a war." ✖

Nick Hilden is a freelance journalist

52(01):14/15|DOI:10.1177/03064220231165367

'Crimea has turned into a concentration camp'

RIGHT: Crimean Tatar activist Nariman Dzhelal, whose essay from prison we publish here

NARIMAN DZHELAL is the leader of the Crimean Tatars, arguably the most persecuted group in Ukraine. He is in jail, but in his essay written from there and published exclusively here, he says he won't let the occupiers break him. Celebrated Ukrainian writer **ANDREY KURKOV** introduces him

NARIMAN DZHELAL WAS born in Uzbekistan where, in 1943, on the orders of Stalin, his father's family was deported from Crimea. His return to his historical homeland, to his native Crimea, was the formative event of his life. He was nine years old when he first saw the Crimean mountains and valleys, when he first set foot on the land of his ancestors.

Dzhelal learnt to read and write before he started school. As a child, he loved to read science fiction. He was fascinated by thoughts of the future. He liked to track how the ideas of old science-fiction writers become reality over time. He also read dystopian novels with great interest, although these novels aroused in him more anxiety about the future than admiration.

He wanted to study law, but by chance he became a student of political science at Odessa University, which he never regretted. After graduating from university, he returned to Crimea, where

They have failed to show the outside world that the Crimean Tatars have come to terms with the annexation

he quickly became a prominent and respected journalist. I remember noticing him for the first time as a talented TV presenter on ART Crimean Tatar Television network.

Dzhelal was also seriously engaged in the political life of the peninsula. The purpose of his activity has always been to improve the life of the Crimean Tatar people, to protect their political and social interests and protect their culture and identity.

After the annexation of Crimea at the end of February 2014, Russia banned the chairman of the Crimean Tatar parliament, Refat Chubarov, and the leader of the Crimean Tatar people, Mustafa Dzhemilev, from entering the territory of the peninsula. Dzhelal, then deputy chairman of the Crimean Tatar parliament, the Mejlis, became the chief representative of the Crimean Tatars. He had a reputation as a very calm and liberal politician, far from radical statements and actions. The Russian authorities hoped to take control of the Mejlis by persuading its leadership to recognise the annexation of Crimea by the Russian Federation. Some of the Crimean Tatar activists agreed to collaborate with the Russian authorities. Dzhelal continued to consider the annexation of Crimea illegal. I have always been struck by his determination to act on his principles and beliefs with a calm understanding that this is the only way to fight injustice and create a path for a positive outcome for the Crimean Tatar people.

In 2016 the Mejlis was banned by

Russian authorities as an extremist organisation. This was followed by regular searches and arrests. Many Crimean Tatar activists were detained or disappeared.

In August 2021, Dzhelal left Crimea for Kyiv for the first meeting of the Crimean Platform, a newly created international organisation whose goal is the de-occupation of Ukrainian Crimea. He must have known what awaited him on his return to Crimea. But he still went to Kyiv and took an active part in the work of the Crimean Platform. The occupying authorities of Crimea could no longer tolerate their ideological enemy. On 4 September 2021 Dzhelal was arrested and charged with an attempted terrorist act.

While in prison, Dzhelal has returned to literature and journalism. He writes articles, poetry and short prose. He also writes letters and I have been in correspondence with him for over a year. He reads a lot. He courageously opposes the Russian authorities, who have failed to break him, which means they have failed to show the outside world that the Crimean Tatars have come to terms with the annexation.

On 21 September 2022 Dzhelal was sentenced to 17 years in prison for a crime he did not commit. This sentence is currently under appeal. There is an urgent need to raise the profile of this case before the final judgment on his appeal, after which he could be transferred to one of most remote Russian prisons and we risk losing touch with him.

CREDIT: Nariman Dzhelal/Facebook

Dignity cannot be annexed

by **NARIMAN DZHELAL**

"TELL ME, WHEN did you get street lighting in your street?" The warden was trying another argument. For more than three weeks I had been undergoing a forensic psychiatric examination in Department 15 of Simferopol's Clinical Psychiatric Hospital. Unlike the pre-trial detention centre, the regime in this institution was more liberal. And sometimes the bored guards started conversations with the "subjects" (the term used for prisoners sent for examination).

For us, such conversations were also one of the few forms of entertainment. They usually began with questions like: "What were you arrested for? How long have you been kept in a pre-trial detention centre?"

"Under what article of law are you being held?"

"Article 281."

"What's that?" (Not every prisoner or warden knows the numbers of Russian laws relating to "political crimes". They are more familiar with the numbers for murder, extortion, robbery, fraud, theft and, of course, 228-I - drugs).

"Sabotage."

"And what did you do?"

"Nothing. But they accused me of blowing up a gas pipeline." →

→   "Oh, the one in Perevalnoye? On the news they said..."

I have had conversations like this countless times. Some of my interlocutors are genuinely interested:

"So if you didn't blow it up, why did they arrest you?"

"I am a journalist."

"Ah! Right!"

Imagine, for many people in Crimea the fact of a journalist being prosecuted for committing a crime is a normal thing. Nobody is even surprised.

More knowledgeable interlocutors (there are not so many of them) end the dialogue differently:

"Do you belong to some organisation?"

"Maybe!" (I wonder what he will say).

"The Mejlis?"

"Exactly!"

"In a leadership position?"

"Bingo!"

"So that's it!"

If time permits and the interlocutor wants to know the details, I explain that, as a journalist and public figure, I opposed the occupation and annexation of Crimea by Russia. For years now, I have written and spoken about human rights violations and political repressions in Crimea, especially the rights of the Crimean Tatar people. And after my trip to Kyiv to attend the Crimean Platform summit, my long-awaited arrest was carried out.

My current interlocutor turned out to be a "tough nut". He tried to argue against me, to show the groundlessness of my position in relation to Russia's actions in Crimea, as usual pointing to the infrastructural changes on the peninsula since 2014:

"When did you get street lighting on your street?"

I wasn't going to fall into his trap. There are two kinds of people. Some evaluate current events through the prism of new street lighting, the construction of an airport, or a road. Thinking with their "bellies", they calmly change one flag for another...

"What are you rocking the boat for?" He had found a stone in the soil of his garden.

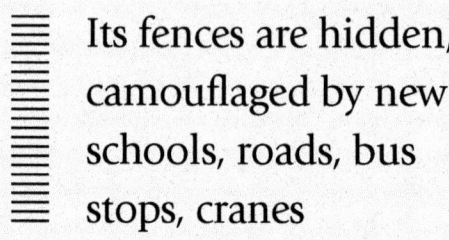

Its fences are hidden, camouflaged by new schools, roads, bus stops, cranes

There are others – perhaps a minority – who give priority to the values of freedom and justice, the opportunity to exercise their rights; to act both according to the law and according to conscience. I try to be that kind of person.

I didn't try to convince my interlocutor. People like him are used to being guided not by principles, but by circumstances. Some cautiously recall how it was before, "under Ukraine". But immediately, as if defending themselves from their "bold" thoughts, as if for the sake of the ubiquitous ears, they talk about how it has become better in Crimea, while the situation in Ukraine, they say, is terrible.

Propaganda categorically invites them to obsequiously think and speak "correctly". Ideas and phrases are so firmly implanted in their heads that even in moments of enlightenment, these ready-made stamps instantly come to their rescue, providing excuses for their unfulfilled expectations.

"Nariman, you remember how, under Ukraine, we kind of started to live well, but then the Maidan ruined everything!"

"Don't confuse cause and effect. The Maidan was a response by a part of Ukrainian society to the policies of President Yanukovych - to wild kickbacks, corruption, to the dominance and nepotism of the "Donetsk elite". Yanukovych openly deceived society by refusing to sign an agreement with the European Union. Society responded accordingly."

"But look what happened to Ukraine! If not for the Maidan, I'm sure life in there would be better now."

"Ukrainians simply did not want and do not want to become a parody of Russia."

It is not easy to argue with such people. They calmly admit that such international crimes as the occupation of a foreign territory, the disregarding of the will of the indigenous people of this territory, the falsification of the will of Ukrainian citizens in Crimea, can be justified by better-lit streets, new roads, schools etc. They have been effectively indoctrinated - taught that the empire brings the light of civilisation to the conquered peoples. The fact that Ervin Ibragimov was kidnapped back in May 2016 and has not yet returned home does not matter to them ...

* * *

"You were warned!" said a strong, rough voice.

A few hours after the search of my house and my arrest, I was sitting on a chair - handcuffed, with a bag over my head - in a basement, no one knows where.

"About what?"

"Not to go to the Crimean Platform."

There it was! Finally, after a rather lengthy conversation about the gas pipeline explosion and my participation in it, I finally heard the real reason for my arrest.

Up to that point, the conversation had been so outlandish, the statements so far-fetched, that I kept waiting for the main point to be voiced.

My attendance at the international summit in Kyiv was certainly not the only reason for my arrest. But more on that later. It was necessary to go to the Crimean Platform, although the risk was higher that year than ever before. The Russian leadership reacted extremely sharply to this event. It was obvious that activists who dared to go from Crimea to Kyiv would attract some serious attention.

Of course, the platform would have taken place without us. The presence at the summit of a handful of people who had come directly from occupied Crimea - formal representatives of the occupied peninsula, living witnesses of what was happening there, participants in peaceful resistance - may have remained unappreciated then, but would acquire significance later. The Kremlin was well aware of this significance and, therefore, did not want anyone to go. We were tailed until we had left Crimea. We were detained on the road, at the border checkpoint where we had a stilted conversation with the border guards.

No one directly said: "Don't go! You'll regret it!". But, apparently, the six-hour grilling was the warning I was now being reminded about.

It didn't stop me.

I had to go for another reason as well. Since 2014, fear had spread throughout Crimea. Using administrative, legislative and informational methods, all residents of Crimea have been taught to refrain from any actions that are not sanctioned by the state, and under no circumstances to go beyond the limits of permitted behaviour. As people succumb to these rigid taboos, they restrain themselves, construct barriers and isolate themselves. Free civic activity, although it had not completely disappeared, had sharply declined, acquiring a sporadic and fragmented character.

It was impossible to remain indifferent to this process. People needed to see examples of different behaviour. Providing such examples was dangerous in the conditions of occupation, but it could inspire hope.

Once, after listening to my friend's emotional speech about his plans to liberate Crimea, it occurred to me that he might not be in time - that there may be no one to liberate. There will be very few people who value freedom and are willing to fight for it, who will continue to see the occupation of Crimea as illegal and who will want it to end. Under the onslaught of propaganda and fear for their safety, they will not only submit to change, they will change themselves.

Few realise that we have actually ended up in a prison, in a kind of concentration camp for the 21st century. Its fences are hidden, camouflaged by new schools, roads, bus stops, cranes towering over new building sites etc. Yet it is a concentration camp with strict rules and cruel guards – where the loyal get treats and the disobedient are punished. In a concentration camp, the goal of the authorities is to turn everyone into a faceless homogeneous mass, absorbing those who disagree or resist ...

We went to the summit so that people could see that it is possible to overcome your fear, to →

PICTURED: Activists protest outside the Russian Embassy in Kyiv against the ill-treatment of Tatars in Russia-occupied Crimea, February 2022

→ act by your principles and beliefs.
Let cautious folk consider us fools!

* * *

"While you were writing your posts on the internet and did not cross the line, no one touched you," said the owner of the rough, strong voice, who talked to me immediately after my arrest.

He came to my room in the FSB office where people under investigation are kept and demanded that I follow him. On the day of my detention, I heard only his voice. I immediately recognised it now. I did not know what place he occupied in the local hierarchy, but he spoke imposingly, with

a sense of superiority. As in the first meeting, he tried to make me feel guilty.

"It was you who dragged the other guys into this story. You messed up their lives." He meant the Akhtemov brothers, Asan and Aziz, who were arrested before me in the same case. According to the text of the accusation, I "recruited" them as saboteurs. Subjected to physical and psychological pressure, both of them "confessed" and made video-recorded statements that they probably read off a prompter.

This video was broadcast by propaganda TV channels. However, as soon as independent lawyers got through to them, they refused to testify and declared that they had been put under psychological and physical pressure.

The words of my interlocutor sounded unconvincing to me. Some of the actions that the investigation attributed to me I did not do at all. And those that I did were motivated by intent that was different from that attributed to me in the investigation.

I had been living on the edge, although it didn't seem to me that I was asking for trouble. How many of my friends and colleagues "crossed" the line and were expelled from Crimea, fined, arrested or even abducted? How many times had my friends and foes been surprised that I was still at large? Some rejoiced, others resented it.

The Crimean Platform had apparently become my "red line". I don't regret crossing it at all. However, I did feel that the criminal prosecution was aimed not only at isolating me and punishing me for my dissent and beliefs; my arrest was also aimed at intimidating everyone who shared my thoughts and acted as I did. What I could not understand was the accusation of sabotage. After all, sabotage did not fit in with my activities. The Kremlin had much more "convincing" grounds for my arrest. For example, membership of the Mejlis of the Crimean Tatar people, which had been banned in Russia since 2016. Or my "calls" to violate the territorial integrity of the Russian Federation. I had said and done many things that had become punishable due to hasty changes to the criminal code made by the State Duma.

It would have been easier for the prosecution to find plausible evidence of those "crimes" since I did not hide my status and public position, and my posts, comments and speeches at events were certainly recorded by authorities.

Of course, in fact, there is no need to prove anything in these investigations. They are traditionally based on the testimony of classified witnesses. And the prosecutor and the judge will once again become accomplices in a crime – the custom-made incrimination of innocent people.

My interlocutor, although I did not understand the purpose of our conversation, was frank: "Do you understand that after your case, the issue of recognising the Mejlis as a terrorist organisation is likely to be raised?"

This revelation did not surprise me. A few hours earlier, lawyers Emine Avamileva and Nikolai Polozov and I had already thought about this threat. The purpose of my arrest was now clear.

The logic was extremely simple. All "leaders of the Mejlis" had now become objects of criminal prosecution by the Russian authorities - Mustafa Dzhemilev, Refat Chubarov, Akhtem Chiygoz, Ilmi Umerov and others. But the FSB needed something dirty, discrediting for their plan. Directly linking the Crimean Tatar's representative body with terrorist actions was just what they needed. Nobody would doubt that these people were inveterate terrorists and that the entire Crimean Tatar people were terrorists.

Very soon the use of the Crimean Tatar people's symbols – the flag and the anthem – could become justification for a further round of political repressions.

Naturally, the Russian authorities would try to use this "achievement" in the international arena as well, discrediting the Crimean Tatar people, its national movement, its representative bodies, leaders and activists - its collective ideas and goals.

However, I know that Russia's lies will not mislead anyone. No one will believe that the Crimean Tatar people, who for many decades have been waging an absolutely non-violent struggle for their fundamental rights, could suddenly descend to primitive and dirty terrorism.

No, the main purpose of this crime - the creation of a new big lie about the small group of indigenous people of Crimea - is the repression of the peninsula itself, its population and the Crimean Tatars.

To commit monstrous crimes – genocide, deportations – it is necessary to inflate political mythology. To justify the mass destruction of people and the creation of concentration camps, you have to come up with a terrible conspiracy of enemies of the people. You have to put the spotlight on a network of vigilant traitors, and create theories of racial inferiority. In today's Russia, a myth has formed about the total threat of terrorism, which has little in common with real global problems.

Crimea has turned into a concentration →

→ camp – a hybrid concentration camp, with the illusion of free life.

* * *

"You will have to follow us now," said the police officer after the search of my house. "Maybe you'll be back in an hour and a half or two."

But he was lying. Consciously or not, I don't know. They put me in a minibus full of FSB officers in balaclavas and took me at high speed to Simferopol. After entering the city, they put a bag over my head and the car went somewhere outside the Crimean capital. It seemed to me, to Bakhchisaray [town in Crimea]. The first informal interviews were held there. I was taken to the FSB office on Franko Boulevard in Simferopol only towards evening.

All that time - until my official arrest in the presence of a lawyer - I clung to the naive hope that they might let me go home. I read about the behaviour of people in a concentration camp in a book by the Austrian psychologist Viktor Frankl. My initial condition was called "admission shock".

Frankl, having experienced all the hardships and horrors of the Nazi camps himself, talks about the life of prisoners, making interesting psychological observations. He offers a way to survive in this hell.

A considerable number of intellectuals and dissidents have compared Russia to a prison. I also drew an analogy between occupied Crimea and a concentration camp. Once in prison, I felt this comparison even more and the observations and conclusions of Viktor Frankl became clearer to me and useful for describing the psychological state of people under occupation.

Most people who end up in concentration camps (or, as in our case, under occupation) are simply not ready for such a striking change in their circumstances - for the brutal trampling of their will and desires, for the restriction on their freedoms. As a result, they experience this shock.

No matter how much I had prepared myself for my possible arrest, the event still put enormous psychological and physical pressure on me. This phenomenon interests me from the point of view of our collective psychology. We need to understand how to better survive the occupation, how to survive in the broadest sense of the word.

Let's remember our condition since 27 February, 2014 – our first reaction to reports about the seizure of the buildings of the Crimean parliament and the takeover of government by Russian military personnel. Wasn't it a shock - especially when as the days went by, total occupation became an inevitable reality?

We were bombarded with contradictory, sometimes incomprehensible information. Many people did not know what to do and were in an extremely difficult psychological state. Hope and despair were fighting inside each of us. There was, at once, the desire to counter the threat – the military columns moving along the highway – and the fear of the machine guns.

In varying degrees of shock, we all entered the concentration camp. Without our consent, without any guilt proven of us, without an investigation or trial, we were placed behind barbed wire, strict new rules were imposed and their prohibitive nature increased from year to year.

Checkpoints appeared on Chongar and Kalanchak [on Crimea's border]. In Crimea, in addition to military guards, a layer of so-called "kapos" quickly formed - voluntary servants from among the prisoners themselves who act as guards.

In terms of psychology, it is at this stage that many prisoners of the newly-created concentration camp experience a state called "pardon delusions". Despite the quite obvious situation and its consequences, people still hope that what is happening around them is some kind of mistake, that salvation will come from

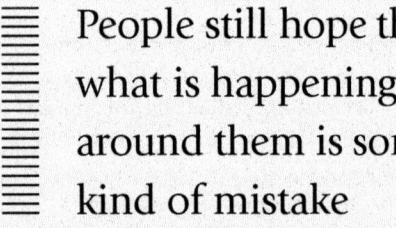

People still hope that what is happening around them is some kind of mistake

somewhere, and the nightmare will end with a joyful awakening.

Remember all those failed predictions about how very soon everything would be resolved – that the world community and Ukraine would not just leave everything as it was – that they would act. Remember all those dashed hopes. Mass betrayal by the employees of the Crimean SBU, police, Ukrainian Armed Forces personnel. All that indecision, concern, impotence...

Although many of my acquaintances were "delirious" with hope even after the first murders, abductions, expulsions and arrests, I tried to look at events realistically and focused on how I was going to live in this concentration camp.

By that time, I had written enough articles about the Russian threat to Crimea and it was unsettling to see how my predictions were becoming a reality.

* * *

In conversations with guards and prisoners, I find one particular quality in many of them that, frankly, irritates me. While they express dissatisfaction with some orders, laws, situations, they never consider the idea of open opposition - of expressing their disagreement.

People don't behave like this by accident. It is the result of many years of systematic work by the current Russian government to suppress society's protest potential and repress any person who does resist.

Since 2014, the people of Crimea have become the object of this multi-purpose work. Many who were punished for disloyalty, disobedience, dissent, openness or courage became either a victim, a prisoner or a hostage of the regime and an instrument through which to influence others. These methods of repression are very similar to those used in prisons and "classical" concentration camps. How many times, especially since 2014, have we, as individuals and as a whole people, experienced a keen sense of injustice? How many accusations and humiliating statements have been and continue to be made against the Crimean Tatars?

But the deepest humiliation was the way that the Russian leadership single-handedly decided the fate of our land, ignoring the opinion of the overwhelming majority of representatives of the indigenous people of Crimea and giving no option but to accept this new status quo. There were those among us who called for humility, for patience. They suggested we silently swallow the humiliation and promised, in return, the solution to certain social problems. Some reproached anyone who thought to oppose occupation, saying that we should not tease a beast that will trample us for disobedience. By saying this, they were already serving the interests of the regime - spreading uncertainty, doubt and fear. Of course, they wanted to protect themselves from repression and they sought to justify their fear: "What did Ukraine ever give you? Why do you so openly and persistently refuse to accept the annexation of Crimea to Russia?"

How many times have I been asked these questions by some (fortunately few) compatriots and Russian journalists? I spare no energy in explaining the obvious: that, firstly, Ukraine is my country – the country in which I grew up, developed as a person, studied, lived, am going to live. And if something is wrong with it, if at some point the country looked at you in the wrong way, this is no reason to leave it, to betray it.

Russia behaved as expected, according to its traditions. It tried to hide its real intentions behind the façade of declarations of adherence to the rules of good neighbourly relations, to the norms of the same international law. In fact, everything turned into aggression and suppression. It is too obvious that the nature of the Russian regime is authoritarian – so alien to us who value freedom, historical memory and the habit of living in a democratic society.

* * *

Some people from the Crimean Tatar community urged others to trust the occupying power, to believe in its promises. Eight years is long enough to see that power's true intentions. Seemingly good actions and decisions had an obvious goal ➔

→ - to consolidate power throughout the territory and over the indigenous people of this fertile land, over the population as a whole. If this goal makes it necessary to build a school, a mosque, a road, they will be built. If this goal is served by financing a "national" TV channel, newspaper and the publication of books, this will be done. Everything remains under vigilant control, and it costs pennies in relation to the country's budget.

The logic of the occupation has been studied and is well known. In the school that was built, our children are taught the history of the metropolis and the "national outskirts" according to retrograde programmes, exclusively in the interpretation of the occupier. Again the aim is to educate loyal citizens. In the newly built mosque, they will praise the mosque, the metropolis, the rulers, and call for obedience and service to them. New roads primarily serve the state's military interests. And the TV channel's obsequious coverage of the authorities' "caring work" contains lies and slander against those who disagree with those authorities.

Clearly, we are only free to fry *chebureki*, dance *haitarma* and demonstrate ostentatious hospitality in front of the "Masters of Crimea" and their satraps at carefully controlled festivals.

This prospect was clear from the outset. Instead of a substantive law on the rehabilitation of the repressed people, providing for, among other things, the restoration of the Crimean Tatar people's national statehood, we were slipped a blank presidential decree. For their 30 pieces of silver, the Kremlin's henchmen began to convince the people that through obedience they would gain incredible benefits.

For their services, these "responsible comrades" thought they would be rewarded with

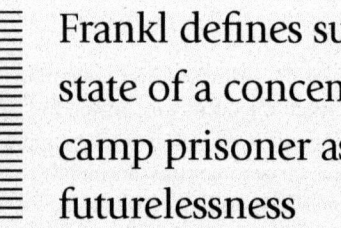

Frankl defines such a state of a concentration camp prisoner as futurelessness

high ranks and excellent wages. Their businesses would not be touched. A blind eye would be turned to incidents of bribery. The prison is now full of those who naively believed that, because of their loyalty, the system would not touch them and that it would not notice corrupt practices and other pranks. Alas!

* * *

Kremlin propagandists keep saying that the occupation of Crimea is irreversible, that it is a fait accompli. Their aim is to deprive us of the will to resist, to show the futility of resisting their monstrous power, to persuade us to be loyal to the occupying power. Like camp guards, they impose on us the absence of an alternative future. Many times, including here in confinement, I have had conversations on this topic.

"Nariman, will we ever see them leave?"

"Undoubtedly! A thief who steals someone else's thing will claim that it is his. But is it so?"

"But they have invested so much in it. Will they leave Crimea just like that?"

"Nobody is saying it will be easy. All honest people will need to put effort into this. However, the course of events that will lead to this result is already clearly visible."

"But when?"

I always answer this question by saying: "Don't ask me when, ask yourself what you did to bring this "when" closer, then it will happen!"

Many doubt their own abilities. Viktor Frankl defines such a state of a concentration camp prisoner as futurelessness. A person who finds himself in the unfavourable conditions of a concentration camp, forced to survive, to endure injustice from the guards, often gives up, especially if he loses his inner support - the idea that his torment, the mockery will end.

Futurelessness dooms the prisoner to a retrospective existence. Choosing to live in the past they do not see themselves, their presence, in the future. As a result, a person cannot find the strength to influence reality. The social reality of the concentration camp seems to a person complete, unchangable and hopeless. Many prisoners simply lay down and die. They do not see the goal or do not believe in it.

Obviously, our concentration camp is different from Frankl's. We are not under direct threat of physical destruction, at least not on the same scale. The absence of a direct threat to life and apparent freedom lulls anxiety and reduces your resistance to the lies that accompany the occupation and political repression. In such deceptively "mild" conditions, many residents of Crimea, even while realising what is happening, prefer to wait it out. They lose their civic activeness and often their faith in a different future. The occupying power encourages this in various ways. We constantly hear maxims that the fate of Crimea has been decided, that Russia will not give it up, that we have no strength to resist, that we need to adapt to the existing situation. We see it on our TV screens. We read about it on the internet. We hear it in conversations.

The flow of information is not haphazard, but carefully formed and controlled – designed to immerse us in a futureless state. What is more, its broadcasters are not only agents of official propaganda, but also our friends, relatives and colleagues, who have succumbed to doubts and unbelief …

As a result, futurelessness, like an infection, begins to spread among more and more people, creating new carriers of this dangerous disease.

There is a cure – strengthening our ideological immunity, maintaining and developing critical thinking, developing the skills needed to think and make decisions on our own, limiting, as far as possible, our exposure to pathogenic propaganda. These means will allow us to defeat this disease sooner or later. Let's not forget that in the context of Crimean Tatar history, any "forever" sounds very funny.

* * *

Seven and a half years passed between the beginning of the Russian occupation and my arrest. All this time I was working in Crimea, although I often thought about leaving. My wife and I discussed it at the very beginning of the

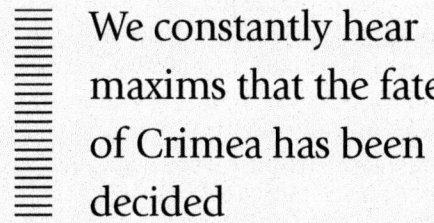

We constantly hear maxims that the fate of Crimea has been decided

occupation. Like many, frightened by Russian aggression, faced with clear threats and imagining potential risks, she asked me if it would be better for us to leave. I reminded her how we cried when snipers were shooting down innocent people on Institutskaya Street, in Kyiv. They were being shot at, but they still went forward. Under fire, they pulled the wounded and dead to safety. We can't leave, I said, and my wife agreed.

When I was in Kyiv, I often went to Institutskaya Street. (I'm told a banner demanding my release and that of the others has recently been hung there.) I tried to understand what pushed those heroes to stand under the bullets. Where did they find the courage? I always returned to Crimea. In that situation, returning was the main decision for me. I set myself the task of acting as long as possible within the frameworks of both the national movement and journalism.

When the Russian authorities tried to show that the inhabitants of Crimea had consented to the so-called annexation, it was extremely important to talk about the complex, contradictory, hybrid reality in which the peninsula had begun to live. Words became my weapon. The written word is clear and penetrates the minds and hearts of people - both in Crimea and beyond. My goal was to inspire, not to let spirits sink or hopes fade away.

I was elected First Deputy Chairman of the Mejlis of the Crimean Tatar people, and Ilmi Umerov was elected Deputy Chairman. The occupier authorities had failed to install their own puppets in the Crimean Tatar parliament.

My rubicon had been crossed. Today we are witnessing a new attempt by the Kremlin to suppress the activities of the Crimean Tatar national movement. But even in adverse, →

→ threatening situations, there is always an opportunity to demonstrate one's dignity, test the firmness of one's convictions and block obviously mean intentions.

Some will say: "Well, look where it got you!". And I say that I am ready to bear the entire burden of responsibility - both for my choice and for my own - for our - struggle. But the actions of one, five, 25 people may not be enough. Our cause will require a critical mass of will and activity from many of us. "How many exactly?" I hear you asking.

*   *   *

When we understand the situation we are in, when we clearly see the cell walls in which our Crimea is enclosed - when the intentions of the guards are obvious - then they do not mislead us. The masks of "guardians of the people's welfare" are torn off and their faces and true motives can be recognised and identified. We have to resist.

Stay…

My first decision was to stay in Crimea. In the homeland I loved with all my heart, which we had recently regained. I dreamed of cherishing her, of growing a beautiful bouquet on her land, as Noman bequeathed. This land is destined to be an oasis of hospitality, not a parade-ground for soldiers' boots and a training ground for tanks. I couldn't leave her like that.

Stay…

My second decision was to be myself, to maintain my beliefs and values. I believe that freedom and democracy are best for human initiative, creativity and the manifestation of positive qualities - freedom and democracy, which are sprouting in Ukraine and are trampled down in Russia. Freedom and democracy can heal the wounds of my people, allow them to rise and fulfill their dream – to freely breathe the air of their native land.

Stay…

The third decision was to stay true to my duty. The duty of a man to whom thousands of Crimean Tatars have delegated the right to speak on their behalf – to offer them a path and be one of the first to follow it. Nine years ago in Khan Saray, I swore to do this and I am sure that I did not break this oath. I am proud that I have been allowed to share responsibility for the fate of my people, for the fate of a free Crimea. And I do not lose hope that my efforts will bear fruit.

These decisions were not easy to make, but they were easy to follow. Because awareness of the correctness of my path never left me; my doubts and hesitations, even when despair came close - there was always someone who said: you have chosen the right direction. And I moved on.

But most of all I was given strength by the people who walked the same path. Some nearby, some at a distance, some who only just set foot on this path.

Stay…

To survive this difficult time, we need to stay true to ourselves, not to give in to false promises. After all, even in this situation of unfreedom, we remain free inside. No one, believe me, no one can take away our inner freedom if we don't give it up ourselves. Here, in a small prison cell, I found confirmation of this. Believe in yourself and your strengths. Rely on your beliefs and those who share them with you.

And do not believe that you are not able to change the situation. Do not believe that you cannot have another future. Viktor Frankl wrote that no one knows his future. No one knows what the next hour will bring him. In the hardships and sufferings that befell our older generation, they were able to see their task, to feel their ability to endure the hardships of deportation. They endured them and returned our homeland to us. They survived the fight against the Soviet empire. They survived deportation, we must survive occupation.

Be yourself and even become stronger and better.

Stay…

I stay with you too! Even while in prison… ✖

Translated by Elizabeth Kourkov

52(01):16/26|DOI:10.1177/03064220231165369

Fighting information termination

JO-ANN MORT explores how the USA's abortion information wars are being fought online

ANYONE SEEKING AN abortion in the USA today is dependent on the laws of the individual states. A new generation of activists is finding creative ways to get the word out regarding rights and access to medical abortions brought about through taking pills, but despite it being against the law to suppress speech or information, regardless of the state's abortion laws, they are running up against censorship issues.

Following the US Supreme Court decision in June 2022 that overturned Roe v Wade and scrapped the federal right to an abortion, the reliance instead on states' laws means 50 sets of regulations regarding abortions across the country. Equally importantly, it also means 50 variants of access to information. This patchwork is profoundly confusing and easily manipulated to the disadvantage of someone seeking an abortion.

A recent Kaiser Family Foundation study shows that many adults in the USA – including women aged between 18 and 49 – are at a loss as to whether medical abortions and emergency contraceptives (the "morning-after pill") are legal in their states.

"In addition, one in eight adults (13%), including one in 10 women, living in states where abortion is currently banned incorrectly believe medication abortion is legal in their state," the report stated.

The majority of abortions in the USA today are medical abortions, but getting hold of the pills used for the procedure — mifepristone and misoprostol — isn't always easy (and the main pill might be outlawed in a number of states). This goes for states with legalised abortions as well as those where abortions are illegal but where people can, in theory, order the pills through the post.

That's where the internet comes in, and where information suppression and misinformation abound. Sites such as the Digital Defense Fund, which offers security and technology resources within the abortion rights movement, and the Electronic Frontier Foundation, which defends digital privacy, try to keep the internet honest about abortion information and how both abortion seekers and medical providers can protect themselves and receive the needed medication. Reddit has also become a go-to for information. But it's a complicated, expansive online universe.

The group Mayday Health, led by Jennifer Lincoln, uses creative communications strategies to publicly share information about abortion pills in areas where abortion is either illegal or restricted. Employing billboards, radio and television adverts and the internet, they reach critical audiences as they figure out how to circumvent suppression attempts.

Mayday Health's public advocacy has faced "truly horrifying attempts to suppress this issue", according to Sam Koppelman, a communications specialist and co-founder of the group. Yet each time Mayday has received a subpoena to take down public billboards, it's responded by adding more.

"We got a subpoena from Mississippi to suppress our billboards. The subpoena was illegally served," Koppelman told Index. "Our lawyers wrote back and said we wouldn't comply."

In addition to the three billboards already up, they added 20.

"These states think they can chill speech by intimidation even though they know they have no case in the courts," he said. "So they probably think that by sending us a subpoena, they can intimidate us into silence." So far, that hasn't worked.

At the University of Idaho, Mayday drove a billboard truck with abortion information across the campus, receiving local news coverage when the university tried to ban it. The organisation repeated this on several other conservative college campuses.

Spotify rejected its ad, so Mayday retaliated. "We put up a playlist of all the [alleged] rapists and sexual predators that Spotify still has on the platform. We posted this on social media. Spotify immediately changed its policy and said they would run our ad," Koppelman said.

"Then, after tons of meetings with their lawyers, they backed off from airing the ads again. So we put the ads on [rival site] Pandora and we reached something like 750,000 people in the targeted states.

"We know that every bit of information we communicate as an educational non-profit is First Amendment protected, we are not going to let any attempts to chill our speech stop us from promoting that message."

People anxious to obtain abortions can be left feeling vulnerable, creating opportunities for anti-abortion activists to prey on them. This is one reason ➔

 Politics and money are at play here in really nefarious and concerning ways

→ the reproductive rights advocate Renee Bracey Sherman started We Testify.

"I shared my story because I didn't hear stories like mine," she told Index of the site. She wanted to erase the stigma and self-censoring which has led to such fear that some people are turning to self-managed care, trying to force a miscarriage. The sacred bond between doctor and patient is being lost, she warned.

Bracey Sherman has also had run-ins with internet platforms. She claims that Twitter attaches warning notices to her feed when she posts about abortion pills. None of her appeals to Twitter has been answered.

Jenna Sherman, programme manager at Meedan's misinformation-busting Digital Health Lab, researches the intersection of technology and reproductive health equity. She and others point to fear of litigation by internet companies as one reason that organisations mark and monitor abortion medical information in a manner that is punitive towards abortion seekers. And, of course, these

Each time Mayday has received a subpoena to take down public billboards, it's responded by adding more

ABOVE: Pro-choice and pro-life activists go head-to-head before the decision to overturn Roe v Wade in Washington, June 2022

companies are money makers who earn more from the highest-paying customers.

Anti-abortion activists are funded by deep-pocketed donors and Sherman said that, as a researcher, she can "follow the money".

"Known perpetrators [of spreading false information] have the largest influence: crisis pregnancy centres, Students for Life of America, Live Action. These organisations are spearheading misinformation claims online and posting the most," she said.

She had been on the website Live Action just before we spoke, and said: "It is chock full of misinformation and they go uncensored. When it comes to abortion, it is really the pro-abortion folks who are getting censored online, not the antis. Politics and money are at play here in really nefarious and concerning ways."

Meanwhile, it's no surprise that the states with the most abortion restrictions are those where more people turn to the internet for information. They are also populations with lower digital and health literacy, making the prevalence of disinformation even more dangerous.

"It is an issue of health justice and basic digital rights and healthcare protections," Sherman stressed. "The internet was a safe place for people on the margins of society to access content in its origins. Now, the internet is a replica of the offline world regarding who gets seen, who is most likely to be harmed."

Accurate information has been protected by internet companies in the past. For example, during Covid companies protected against misinformation.

In January, the FDA – the agency that oversees prescription drugs across the USA – made abortion pills available in chain pharmacies. But this protocol isn't available to those in the most restrictive abortion law states. That's one reason why abortion providers are switching to use a new protocol with just the single pill – misoprostol – which can often be obtained easily without a prescription. This drug, when used in lesser doses, is used to treat ulcers. But it has proven to be effective on its own to terminate pregnancies. It's all part of the race as science tries to outrun censorship in the ongoing heated US abortion war. ✖

Jo-Ann Mort is a USA-based journalist

52(01):27/29|DOI:10.1177/03064220231165376

Keeping track of privacy concerns

When Roe v Wade was overturned last summer, people across the USA were justifiably worried about what it would mean not just for reproductive rights but for privacy more generally. In Virginia, for example, this February a bill to prevent the ability of law enforcers to obtain private menstrual records of women has been struck down. Republican Governor Glenn Youngkin thwarted attempts to pass the bill in the Democrat-led state senate. The bill would have stopped police being able to issue search warrants for menstrual data stored in tracking apps on mobile phones or other electronic devices. Despite half the chamber's Republicans supporting the bill, Youngkin killed it through a procedural move in a subcommittee of the Republican-controlled House.

Youngkin's actions follow a failed attempt in January to ban abortion after 15 weeks with exceptions, down from 26 weeks and 6 days, by Republicans in the Virginian senate.

One state across, in Florida the High School Athletic Association is currently floating the idea of female high school athletes recording their menstrual cycle histories and submitting them to their schools. According to the committee collecting such information is simply good practice for monitoring girls' physical health because period abnormalities can be, they say, a sign of "low energy availability, pregnancy, or other gynecologic or medical conditions". That wording alone is deeply suspicious.

It's no wonder in this climate that women across the USA have been deleting period apps en masse. Even before the overturning of Roe v Wade, women had concerns about these apps. It wasn't until 2021 that Flo, one of the most popular, agreed to obtain user permissions before sharing personal health information, after reaching a settlement with the Federal Trade Commission. From 2016 to 2019, the company passed on certain health details of its users to technology firms.

A race to the bottom

Corruption is corroding the once-democratic Peru. As people take to the streets, **SIMEON TEGEL** reports on the role of politicians and the media

THE MOOD WAS festive as night began to fall and the anti-government protesters marched towards central Lima chanting and waving banners, says Peruvian journalist Pao Ugaz. That was when the riot police chose to act. First, they fired teargas into the peaceful crowd. Then heavily armed officers moved in, beating protesters and the handful of accompanying journalists alike, including Ugaz. Although she frantically waved her press credentials at them, one officer pushed her against a wall and repeatedly punched her.

Eventually, Ugaz and dozens of others escaped the unprovoked assault by jumping over a wall into an underpass 12 feet below. Miraculously, no one was seriously injured from the drop.

"Police don't act that way in a democracy," said Ugaz, 49, a prominent print journalist and TV anchor known in Peru for her reporting about child abuse in a Catholic lay group.

"I don't know what their orders were, but the officers who attacked us were in 'Vietnam' mode. They weren't listening or even thinking. They just wanted to hurt people."

Despite its brutality and the way journalists and other citizens were set upon by security forces, there was nothing out of the ordinary about the incident that took place on 4 February in Peru's current febrile, polarised climate.

Peru's democracy has been in trouble for a while now

Since president Pedro Castillo was impeached and arrested on 7 December for attempting to shutter Congress and rule by decree – in a desperate, botched effort to escape anti-corruption prosecutors – some 40 protesters have been shot dead by police, while dozens of journalists have been physically attacked, some by demonstrators and some by members of the PNP, the national police force.

The use of state force comes amid a rapid deterioration in civil liberties and free speech as a weak government responds to a crisis of legitimacy with what critics categorise as paranoid repression. In doing so, it has been cheered on by much of Peru's highly-concentrated mainstream Lima-based media, who have joined with authorities in stigmatising the protesters, who principally come from impoverished Andean communities. They've been labelled "terrorists" – a term with particularly heavy baggage in Peru, where the Maoist insurgents of Shining Path killed an estimated 31,000 people during the 1980s and 1990s.

Under the guise of stopping terrorism, riot police have used an armoured troop carrier to smash their way into Lima's San Marcos University, the oldest university in the Americas, to arrest 194 protesters before – in the absence of incriminating evidence – being forced to release all but one without charge.

Prosecutors have also been raiding left-wing activists' homes, citing the possession of books by Karl Marx, among others, as evidence of illegal activity, and have set up a "terrorist" hotline for the public to denounce supposed subversives. They have been seeking up to three years in pre-trial

ABOVE: People say goodbye to dozens of dead after heavy clashes with police during protests by government opponents.

detention for protest organisers found to have raised a few hundred dollars to pay for the medical treatment of injured protesters – this despite failing to interview police and army officers involved in the killings of demonstrators.

Many serious voices are now warning that the government of Castillo's

CREDIT: Denis Mayhua/dpa/Alamy

constitutional but deeply unpopular successor, Dina Boluarte, is democratic in name only. Indeed, in February, the Economist Intelligence Unit published its annual Democracy Index, recategorising Peru from an "imperfect" democracy to a "hybrid" democratic-authoritarian regime. The decline in the country's ranking was based on the events of 2022, when Castillo was still president; in other words, even before the latest turmoil and crackdown took place.

Meanwhile, a presenter on state-owned TVPeru, Carlos Cornejo, has been fired apparently for noting that it was police who killed a demonstrator in Lima, and the government has presented a bill that would require journalists covering the protests to register with authorities and "support" the police. The mayor of Lima has also banned protests in the city centre, a glaring violation of the constitution.

Throughout it all, a far-right group calling itself the Resistance has repeatedly harassed journalists and activists viewed as progressive, including chanting anti-Semitic slurs outside the house of investigative reporter Gustavo Gorriti, without the police or prosecutors taking action.

Peru's democracy has been in trouble for a while now. Most commentators date the start to 2016, when Keiko Fujimori, daughter of the jailed hard-right 1990s strongman Alberto →

Police have assaulted reporters and photographers from Peru's 'alternative' media

→ Fujimori, refused to accept her narrow loss in the presidential election. Fujimori, who is facing her own corruption trial and potentially lengthy prison sentence, then proceeded to use her majority in Congress to launch a sustained assault on governance and the rule of law, bringing down two presidents, Pedro Pablo Kuczynski and Martín Vizcarra, in the process.

It was amid this chaos that Castillo, a little-known rural schoolteacher and former wildcat strike leader, snatched a surprise win in the 2021 presidential race. The win raised the hopes of many of Peru's most marginalised citizens, with a raft of populist and frequently improbable promises. That was when things really took a turn for the worse for Peruvian democracy, the country's journalists and the shared national understanding of the basic facts regarding the Andean nation's political and social divisions.

The leftist dark horse, who had no prior experience of elected office, packed his cabinet and government agencies with unqualified and frequently corrupt apparatchiks from his Free Peru party, whose self-declared Marxist-Leninist manifesto warned that the press could never be free under the "yoke of capitalism". They included several with a history of glorifying Shining Path, and one even alleged to have been a bombmaker for the group.

Throughout his chaotic 17 months in office, Castillo routinely vilified the media, calling journalists a "joke" and claiming that they were "paid" to criticise him. He also stopped giving

press conferences and only rarely gave interviews, usually to sympathetic outlets, after a catastrophic interview on CNN in February 2021.

At the same time, the ultra-conservative majority in Congress, which repeatedly sought to impeach Castillo but aligned with him on two issues (their shared opposition to anti-corruption measures and hostility to the media) banned journalists from the legislative chamber and sought to criminalise the publishing of leaked official information. As both the president and lawmakers staggered from one ethical scandal to another, the atmosphere became more and more heated.

It eventually boiled over under Castillo's estranged former vice-president, Boluarte, as she stepped in to replace him after his 7 December act of political seppuku. Despite having run on the same Free Peru ticket, she swiftly moved to shore up her own position, including heading off a potential ideologically driven impeachment, by swerving to the right and aligning with the congressional majority.

Switching from Marxism-Leninism, at least on paper, to Peru's Trumpian hard right may seem improbable, but in the country's dysfunctional, opportunistic and venal politics, it is par for the course. Self-interest typically overrides principles to the point where politicians changing parties multiple times even has its own name: *transfuguismo*. Among other things, Boluarte's metamorphosis meant responding to the inevitable protests at Castillo's ouster with an iron fist, sending in the armed forces and riot police to use lethal force against the demonstrators. While some of them were behaving violently, many were simply exercising their constitutional right to peaceful protest.

The result has been two massacres – first when 10 protesters were shot dead in the southern mountain region of Ayacucho, and then when 18 were killed in the neighbouring Puno region. Boluarte has claimed she wants

"dialogue" with the protesters and yet insists the police's handling of the demonstrations has been "immaculate" – even claiming, with zero evidence, that the dead were shot by other protesters using "dumdum" bullets smuggled from Bolivia. (Peruvian media has revealed that most of the autopsies found wounds compatible with PNP ammunition.) The bloodshed has cost Boluarte her legitimacy, with 75% of Peruvians now wanting her to force new elections by resigning. Congress is even more loathed, with its disapproval rating hovering near 90%.

All the while, journalists continue to be caught up in the crossfire – sometimes literally. Initially, it was those from Lima's largely conservative mainstream media being targeted by Castillo supporters in protests in impoverished Andean regions, as Peru's racial, cultural and geographic fault lines translated into tensions between the capital's biggest news brands and the largely rural citizens whose hopes Castillo had raised and dashed.

But as the turmoil wore on and the protests moved to Lima, those attacking journalists were increasingly the security forces. Above all, police have assaulted reporters and photographers from Peru's "alternative" media, who frequently report via YouTube and other online platforms. These new outlets are now home to many of the country's best journalists. They've been squeezed out of Peru's traditional media, dominated by the El Comercio Group, whose newspapers have captured 80% of Peru's newspaper readership.

The National Association of Journalists of Peru has documented dozens of such attacks. Its executive director, Zuliana Lainez, says the attacks frequently happen despite journalists being identified as press, including with marked vests and helmets.

"The police absolutely cannot argue that they didn't know," Lainez told Index. "There has not even been a press release from the police or interior

ABOVE: Dina Boluarte at the swearing-in ceremony of the president at Congress in Lima, December 2022

minister, nothing, to say it was a mistake or 'We are investigating'. The police have not even tried to deny that this is a policy. It's clear that they have the approval from above."

Lainez also emphasises how some of the Lima-based media's heavily slanted coverage, often tinged with racial condescension towards Andeans, has stoked the tensions and created a vicious circle of biased coverage and ignorance of the rural communities that are protesting.

"Journalists in the provinces are fed up with the Lima media, because they are now being accused of being part of a supposedly corrupt, biased press," she said, adding: "The big media and Lima have never engaged in self-criticism.

That allows news editors to say 'I can't send a team to those protests. They'll just get beaten up'. And then they don't cover the protest, and the right to information is being affected."

For Ugaz, fighting for serious journalism in this challenging environment is nothing new. Indeed, she has for years been the target of sustained legal harassment as allies of her various reporting subjects have misused Peru's criminal defamation laws and other statutes in their attempts to silence her. The accusations have typically been absurd to the point of surreal, including claims that she has been clandestinely marketing uranium from deposits in the Andes.

"In any other jurisdiction, these cases would have been thrown out by the judge before they even started," said Ugaz. "But in Peru, I am being continually pursued. It's a message to

other journalists not to go after powerful people. When you get investigated for corruption, however crazy and baseless the accusations, people think, 'Well, she must've done something'."

Fernando Tuesta, a leading Peruvian political scientist and former head of Peru's electoral agency, has also been the target of defamation campaigns on one of the country's main TV stations, Willax, which churns out right-wing disinformation, for his analysis of political corruption and proposals for reform.

"Good people no longer want to go into politics," he said. "Politics here has become almost exclusively this realm of opportunists and corrupt adventurers."

Based on current trends, the same may also soon apply to journalism in Peru. ✖

Simeon Tegel is a journalist based in Lima

52(01):30/33|DOI:10.1177/03064220231165377

When comics came out

SARA CENTURY explores the landscape of suppression that eventually gave way to a new era of queer comics, and why the censors are still fighting back

THE IMAGE OF the comic book community has long been associated with cultural spoofs such as the Comic Book Guy from The Simpsons, an unnecessarily rude shop owner who seems to love the act of gatekeeping more than the comics themselves. The stereotype isn't totally unfounded, but comics have always had a much more complex readership with more varying subject matter than they're given credit for, and that's truer now than ever.

In the USA, the medium hit record sales in 2021 and, as their popularity continues to grow, censors are increasingly agitated by their subject matter, seeking to pull seminal graphic novels and newer works alike from the shelves. In the wider landscape for book bans across the USA, books by queer

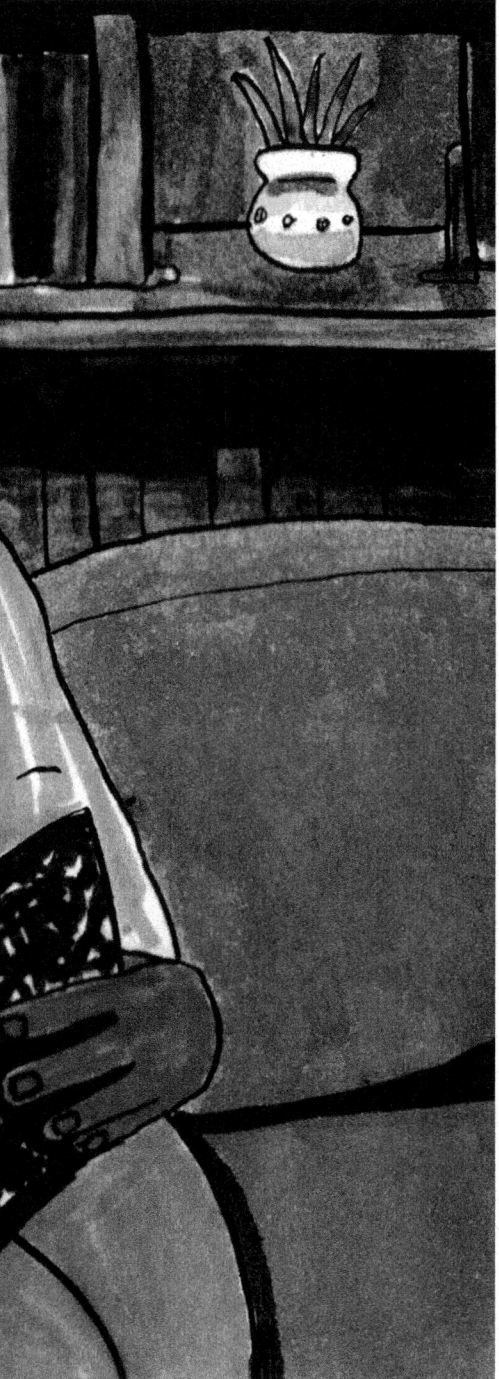

Comic resistance

From the get-go superheroes were a response to oppression. **FRANCIS CLARKE** writes on their early Jewish origins

Superman
First appearing on the cover of Action Comics #1, some may think the root of the character lay in Friedrich Nietzsche's conceiving of the Übermensch, distorted later into the Nazi belief of an Aryan master race. However, creators Jerry Siegel and Joe Shuster, who turned to the comic book industry after facing anti-Semitism as writers and artists, chose Moses as the basis for Superman. With his birth name Kal-El, the suffix El meaning "God" in Hebrew, Superman's later importance as an inspiring symbol beating Nazi agents led to Joseph Goebbels angrily denouncing him.

Captain America
Created by Jewish artists Joe Simon and Jack Kirby in 1940, Captain America is defiantly anti-fascist. The Anglo-named Steve Rogers was initially frail and weak, with the serum injected to create his famed alter-ego created by Dr Joseph Reinstein. The Jewish character pounded Adolf Hitler on the cover of his first comic and had the Nazi agent Red Skull as his enduring archenemy. In an imaginary world, at least, Jewish people were successfully fighting back.

Batman
Arguably the biggest superhero of all, Batman debuted in 1939's Detective Comics #27. Artist Bob Kane and writer Bill Finger were both of Ashkenazi Jewish descent, and Detective Comics was owned by two Jewish entrepreneurs, Harry Donenfeld and Jack Liebowitz. While Batman failed to have the same overt Jewish influence as Superman and Captain America, the push of Jewish artists, writers and entrepreneurs to the US comic books sector in the 1930s ensured a truly iconic character was born.

creators made up a whopping 41% of the challenged materials between July 2021 and July 2022. Comics are at the centre of the conversation, with Maia Kobabe's graphic memoir Gender Queer cited by PEN as the most commonly banned book in the last school year.

Jennifer Camper, a long-time comic creator and founding director of the Queers & Comics conference, believes that the censors' focus on queer comics is no accident, and that with increased visibility comes a backlash.

"Conservatives are still trying to censor queer content, and queer cartoonists, especially trans cartoonists, are threatened with violence and online harassment," she said.

According to Camper, the fact that the medium is often considered a lower art form by both the general public and critics may be a major part of why conservatives find comics especially threatening.

"Censors attack comics because words and pictures hit the reader in an intimate and visceral way," Camper said. "Comics are very open and accessible to readers, and people approach comics easily. The same narrative that's presented in a comics format might be overlooked if it were presented in prose, in a film or in a painting."

Cartoonist MariNaomi has long been a fixture in indie and underground comics and zines, but last year they came under fire for their book Losing the Girl from the Life on Earth series. These books were called into question in Texas for queer subject matter and removed from the shelves.

MariNaomi told Index: "I used to joke that I wanted my books to be banned, for the cred, but when it happened I just felt sad. I was lucky that my banned book made the Los Angeles Times, and essentially revitalised my book sales. Most books get banned →

Before, a creator being out was potentially career-ending

➔ quietly. Presumably the careers of the quiet-banned authors just fade away."

In the USA, comics and censors have been at odds with one another for as long as the medium has existed. Fredric Wertham's 1954 book Seduction of the Innocent – a psychological study of anecdotal evidence of the mental toll reading comics might have on children – is widely derided today for its role in causing nationwide moral panic, covered extensively in David Hajdu's book The Ten-Cent Plague.

Wertham was fixated on homoerotic subtext in superhero comics. In the decades since, many have wholeheartedly agreed with his assertions, but have found them a cause for celebration rather than censorship. Jill Lepore's The Secret History of Wonder Woman reveals that Wertham's accusations of lesbian subtext in the series were likely intentional on the part of the creator, though the implication that this was a potentially civilisation-wrecking travesty is perhaps over-reactive.

These were comics made by LGBTQ cartoonists for the queer community, comics that did not cater to mainstream heterosexual opinion

Even today, book bans are compared to the mass hysteria that followed Seduction of the Innocent, which resulted in two days of hearings by the Senate Judiciary Committee to Investigate Juvenile Delinquency in 1954. In the immediate aftermath of the Senate Comic Book Hearings that put publishers on trial and saw nationwide comic book burnings came a complicated, self-imposed code of conduct known as the Comics Code Authority. It began stamping its seal on the covers of most comics, continuing to do so for decades.

The Underground Comix scene of the 1960s, subverting the mainstream press with X-rated content, rose to challenge the restrictive code – but it was criticised for its overt sexism and racism. In response, a further movement came hot on its heels and is often forgotten by history: the Wimmen's Comix series by Trina Robbins and others, working to establish women creators as equally talented and worthy of notice.

"Most of the early underground work was by het-cis [heterosexual cis-gendered] whiteboys — hell, mostly all the arts and media were created by het-cis whiteboys," Camper explained. "People of colour, queers and women were frustrated by that, and that need to tell our own stories launched new comics."

Wimmen's Comix featured Robbins's story Sandy Comes Out, often regarded as the first story about a lesbian to appear in a North American comic. In 1973, creator Mary Wings released Come Out Comix, wanting to offer a similar narrative but from the perspective of an out lesbian rather than an ally such as Robbins. Other queer underground comix followed, such as Roberta Gregory's Dynamite Damsels.

However, perhaps no comic was more influential than the long-running Gay Comix. It was launched in 1980, first through Kitchen Sink Press and then through Bob Ross, initially helmed by the late Howard Cruse (who was succeeded by Robert Triptow and Andy Mangels). According to Camper, Cruse – also a cartoonist – is rightfully regarded as the godfather of queer comics.

"He created a community for many LGBTQ cartoonists, including myself. The comics published in Gay Comix were new and exciting because they were queer, truthful and unapologetic,"

she said. "These were comics made by LGBTQ cartoonists for the queer community, comics that did not cater to mainstream heterosexual opinion."

Though Gay Comix ran for only 25 issues until 1998, it featured a number of the era's most important queer creators, including Alison Bechdel, who was at the time best known for the syndicated comic strip Dykes to Watch Out For. This period saw queer comics undergo a revolution towards visibility. Before, a creator being out was potentially career-ending. By the end of the Gay Comix run, major strides had been made, with openly LGBTQ+ creators such as Phil Jimenez helming high-profile books for DC. The era might not have eradicated the stigma around hiring queer creators but it certainly challenged it.

The last two decades have seen explosive growth in terms of diversity of readership and subject matter in comics. Though major queer superheroes such as Iceman and Batwoman often dominate the news cycle, more personal works such as George Takei's They Called Us Enemy and Trung Le Nguyen's The Magic Fish have topped bestseller charts.

Book bans challenge this newfound access. After Losing the Girl came under attack, MariNaomi noted that the increased sales were a double-edged sword. The people showing support generally already had access to their books, rather than making new discoveries in libraries. During a recent panel, they said: "What I really want is for some kid who's going through a hard time to be able to go into the school library and pick up the book and see that other people might have gone through what they're going through and not feel so alone."

MariNaomi believes that US culture and media around queerness is shifting, particularly amongst young people. They told Index: "I believe that the folks who are intent on censoring queer works are motivated as a pushback to that, but that's obviously not going to fly."

In the end, perhaps the targeting

of queer comics by conservatives is a response to the same thing that draws so many queer readers and creators to the medium – the sense that just by reading they become a part of the larger history and community of queer comics. ✖

Sara Century is a comic creator, writer and co-host of the Bitches on Comics podcast. She created the illustrations for this article

52(01):34/37|DOI:10.1177/03064220231165378

IRAN SPECIAL

In Iran women's bodies are the battleground

Reflecting on the recent protests, **KAMIN MOHAMMADI** writes about growing up in the Shah's Iran where women were told to de-robe, and the terrible u-turn after

T'S BEEN SIX months since images poured out of Iran that took the world by surprise: young women burning their headscarves and cutting off their hair at street protests in what looked like a conflagration of fury.

In the Islamic Republic of Iran, where Sharia laws demand that women be covered up with hijabs, these were potent acts – not just illegal but liable to expose the women to arrest and even death. Protests at the abusive treatment of women, minorities and students have become commonplace in recent years, but never before have women shed their headscarves and burnt them in public in such a show of pure rage.

The protests erupted spontaneously after the death of Mahsa Jina Amini, a 22-year-old Iranian Kurd who died while in police custody after being arrested for "improperly" wearing her hijab. The Kurdish freedom cry of "Woman, Life, Freedom" has since become the dominant chant.

While the brutal treatment of Amini was the spark, the real heat comes from

What is happening in Iran is the frontline of feminism today

decades of oppression of any viable opposition to the hardline clerical regime, a free-falling economy, mass corruption, and disgust at the hypocrisy of the ruling elite. This elite refuses to engage with Iranians' simplest demands, even as their own children post pictures of their luxurious, scantily-clad lives on social media. They enjoy the pilfered resources of our country while ordinary Iranians struggle to make ends meet with multiple jobs and frequent power outages in the freezing winter.

The headscarf being waved by Iranian women is, for the young people of the country, no longer anything to do with Islam but a symbol of regime oppression.

The women of Iran have been demanding their rights ever since Ayatollah Khomeini took power in 1979. The first demonstration against the mandatory wearing of the hijab took place just three weeks after Khomeini's arrival. Before the revolution, Iranian women had some of the most liberal laws in the Middle East: they had been voting since 1964 and had equal rights to divorce and custody of children. The marriage age for girls was 18.

I grew up in Iran in the 1970s and lived in a world in which my mother and aunties wore what they liked (mostly mini-skirts) and where they fully expected that we, the young girls, would go to university and work when we grew up. The Shah's father had

forcibly unveiled women in the 1930s, a top-down imposition of his modernising values which meant that many conservative women preferred to stay at home than appear in public "naked". But for many others, the policies of Reza Shah, and subsequently his son, were liberating – allowing women to attend university and work outside the home, bringing literacy even to rural areas.

And with the implementation of the Shah's White Revolution in the early 1960s, women were given the vote. This was the first time that Khomeini, then an important cleric and religious scholar, denounced the Shah's policies – in particular with regards to women's liberation. Giving women the vote was, he said, tantamount to prostitution. Khomeini was jailed by the Shah and finally sent into exile.

Perhaps it should be no surprise that the first thing Khomeini did after taking power in 1979 was to repeal the Family Act of 1976 – the most progressive in the region – and plunge the marriage age for girls to nine. It now stands at 13 after decades of activism by Iranian women.

The fact that women in Iran enjoy the right to work and vote and appear in public spaces is testament to their relentless fight for their rights in the Islamic Republic.

Of Iran's population of 87 million people, with a literacy rate of over 86%, women make up 65% of university graduates. But these are people whose word in court is worth half that of a man, and who cannot sing, dance or show their hair or body in public.

Significant uprisings in Iran led by women have taken place since that first Women's Day march in March 1979, most notably in 1999, 2005, 2009 and in 2017 – the Girls of Revolution Street protests – when Vida Movahedi stood silently on the street with her head uncovered and her headscarf held out on a stick, inspiring other women to do the same. Some 29 people were arrested but it happened again in 2019, when

Never before have women shed their headscarves and burnt them in public in such a show of pure rage

the regime blacked out the internet and 1,500 protesters were killed.

Of the most recent protests, doctors and nurses have reported that security forces target women protesters' faces, genitals and breasts when shooting at them, while male protesters are shot in the legs and arms. And yet Iranian women are not cowed; there are increasing instances of civil disobedience including going about their daily lives without the hijab. And in spite of four executions – and many more protesters condemned to be killed – the courage and bravery of ordinary people in Iran continues to drive this movement forward and keep the protests alive.

Whatever happens now, the protests show that Iran and its people will never be the same again. After decades of trying to reform the regime and its more repressive laws, they now want nothing short of regime change, and the protests are morphing into new forms of civil disobedience and online activism as well as protests and strikes.

And these protests have significance beyond Iran's borders. Already the women of Afghanistan are protesting against the Taliban's discrimination and openly naming their Iranian sisters as inspiration.

Last December, when the Taliban banned women from attending university, Afghan women turned out to protest in force the next day, citing the Woman, Life, Freedom movement, and men in Afghanistan committed acts of civil disobedience in solidarity with the female

ABOVE: A protest takes place in Los Angeles in solidarity with protesters in Iran

protesters, emulating Iranian men. About 50 male university professors resigned their positions, while some male students reportedly refused to sit their exams.

What is happening in Iran today is the frontline of feminism – young women taking back the right to their space and bodily autonomy, even at the cost of their lives. And, given the global assault on women's rights, this is a struggle that touches us all. ✖

Kamin Mohammadi is author of The Cypress Tree: A Love Letter to Iran

52(01):38/39|DOI:10.1177/03064220231165379

☩HURST

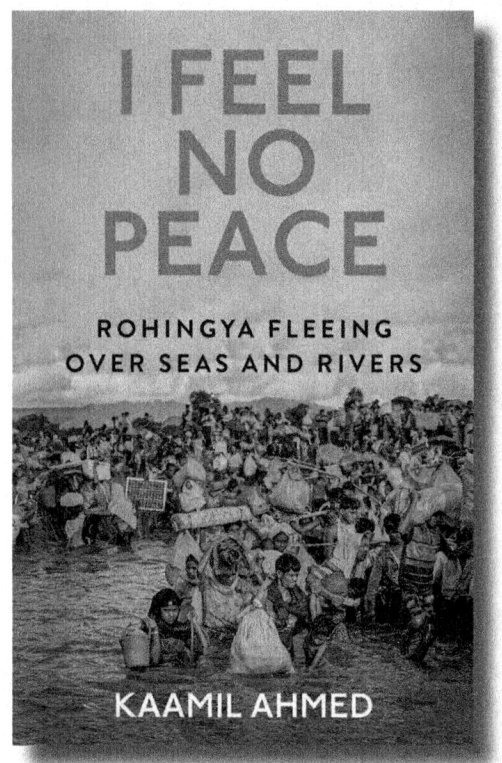

'This book goes to the heart of the eternal and under-reported suffering of the Rohingya. . . An important story of our times.' — **Jon Snow**

'While documenting the harm done by the UN and the Bangladeshi state, Ahmed humanises those normally dehumanised—the refugees.' — **Aditya Chakrabortty**, *The Guardian*

'A haunting and poetic, yet incisive and grounded, account of the tragedies that have befallen the Rohingya, of the realities of a people living almost entirely in exile, and of their struggles to maintain dignity and hope in the face of persecution and betrayal.' — **Kenan Malik, author, broadcaster and *Observer* columnist**

Rohingya men, women and children have been fleeing their homes for forty years. With the Rohingya almost entirely in exile, *I Feel No Peace* is the first book-length exploration of their lives abroad, drawing on hundreds of hours of interviews and long-standing relationships within the diaspora. Kaamil Ahmed speaks to the families of snatched children, and people kidnapped to feed the human trafficking nourished by Rohingya suffering. Most disturbingly, he reveals the complicity of NGOs and the UN in the refugees' plight. But Ahmed also uncovers resilience and hope; stories of how a scattered community survives. The lives uncovered in *I Feel No Peace* are complex, heart-breaking and unforgettable.

9781787389311 | £18.99 hb

Kaamil Ahmed is a journalist at *The Guardian*, covering international development, who previously lived in and reported from Jerusalem, Bangladesh and Turkey. Kaamil was born in East London and studied at Queen Mary University of London. This is his first book.

IRAN SPECIAL

Face to face with Iran's authorities

The award-winning war correspondent **RAMITA NAVAI** tells **MARK FRARY** about the time she was detained in Tehran, what the current protests mean and her Homeland cameo

PICTURED: Journalist Ramita Navai, who has lived and worked in Iran. She feels there is "no turning back" from the current protests

CREDIT: Graeme Robertson

T IS EARLY 2020 and a small group of reporters is being briefed by a national security adviser to the US president on negotiations with the Taliban. One of the reporters doubts the positive spin on how the negotiations are going and requests an off-the-record comment. The reporter asks the adviser what he sees as the main obstacle to a deal.

"America hasn't got a whole lot of good options. We are not staying forever; the president has made that abundantly clear. We can't just walk away either."

"Why not?" asks the reporter.

The adviser replies: "Our forces pass a critical point and Kabul falls in six weeks."

A year later, following the withdrawal of US troops, Kabul falls, not in weeks but days.

This press conference never actually took place – it is a scene from the final season of the political drama Homeland. The security adviser is actor Mandy Patinkin, playing the gruff but principled Saul Berenson. The reporter playing opposite Patinkin, however, is real.

"Homeland likes to use real people and they wanted real foreign correspondents," said British-Iranian investigative journalist and documentary maker Ramita Navai. "I had to audition for it and got the role as a foreign correspondent being briefed on Afghanistan, about negotiations with the Taliban for an American withdrawal. It was prophetic; two years later, I would be in Afghanistan covering the aftermath of that."

Navai didn't let on to Homeland's producers that she was a huge fan →

They took me to an abandoned warehouse with broken windows and flexes hanging from the ceiling

→ of Patinkin, and one of his much earlier roles in particular, that of the swordsman Inigo Montoya in the cult movie The Princess Bride. She admits to being too star-struck to tell Patinkin and it was left to one of her journalist colleagues, David Loyn, who also has a brief part in the show, to let him know.

"We were having a break between camera changes and Mandy called over to me and said "Ramita, sit next to me". I was so excited he knew my name. My heart was beating very fast and he said he had something to tell me. His bushy beard pressed against my cheek and he whispered in my ear: 'Hello. My name is Inigo Montoya, you killed my father, prepare to die'".

Fans of the The Princess Bride will know just how iconic this line is.

Navai told Index: "I died and went to heaven."

Appearing in Homeland is light relief for a journalist who is usually on the small screen in her own documentaries, covering subjects such as blood diamonds in Zimbabwe, sex trafficking in Mexico, the war in South Sudan, child prisoners in Burundi and migrant torture camps in Egypt for Channel 4's Unreported World. Since then she has made a number of documentaries for PBS Frontline, and won an Emmy award for Syria Undercover in 2012.

2022's No Country for Women for ITV is the result of a six-month investigation into the Taliban's treatment of women, exposing mass arrests and abductions. It won the Grierson Award for Best Current Affairs Documentary, as well as a Rose d'Or Award.

In addition to her documentaries, Navai is the creator and host of The Line of Fire podcast, which made the top 10 in the Apple podcast charts, and

features one-on-one interviews with war correspondents. It featured Afghani journalist Shoaib Sharifi, as well as CNN's Clarissa Ward. A second series is out soon.

"When you are in the flow of the conversation people open up and share stuff they have never shared before. That is why I love podcasts. It feels like an intimate thing. You are listening to voices and it is as though people are sitting next to you. The next series, we are going to open it up to people who are not just war correspondents. I was really mindful that people did not feel it was just a load of war correspondents patting themselves on the back. It was important to have people who live in the countries they report from rather than those who helicopter in and out. These are always the unsung journalists who are at most risk."

Her native Iran is never far from her thoughts.

She was born in Tehran but left with her family when the Islamic Revolution happened in 1979. Her 2014 book City of Lies, which won her the Royal Society of Literature's Jerwood Award for non-fiction, tells the stories of ordinary Iranians forced to live extraordinary lives: the porn star, the ageing socialite, the assassin and enemy of the state who ends up working for the Republic, the dutiful housewife who files for divorce, and the old-time thug running a gambling den.

Tehran, the City of Lies of the title, is described with romantic nostalgia but rails against the hypocrisy of the regime.

"This is one of many reasons that Iranians have had enough," said Navai of the current protests wracking Iran. "The regime is not only corrupt politically, it is corrupt morally. While

the state enforces laws that govern its citizens' most intimate affairs, meanwhile people in power do as they please. You have people in power whose children are partying in Iran and across the world, doing drugs, wearing whatever they want and having normal sexual relations that are not allowed under the regime. It is this hypocrisy that people are finally fed up with."

Up to 20,000 people have now been detained as a result of the protests that erupted in Iran last September. Those arrested have been subject to physical and psychological torture, rape and been made to make forced confessions. Some, including 22-year-old Mahsa (Jina) Amini whose death sparked the current protests, have died in custody, while four have been executed for their role in the protests.

Navai knows only too well what those who have been detained are facing. She has been detained by the Iranian authorities several times over the years. She says her first arrest came just after she had started working as Tehran correspondent for The Times and was covering the anniversary of the Islamic Revolution.

"I was at a rally with a lot of other journalists and I was interviewing some Iranians. Before I knew it, two undercover intelligence agents had taken me away; none of my colleagues saw me being taken. It was a terrifying experience. They took me to an abandoned warehouse with broken windows and flexes hanging from the ceiling and there was an armed man standing outside the room. They took all my possessions and carried a table and chairs into the room before starting with a good cop/bad cop routine. It was very manipulative psychologically and was designed to break me. They started telling me that I had been asking anti-revolutionary questions and said I had been telling people how to answer. It was all lies but I was utterly unprepared for this."

Her interrogators asked her whether

RIGHT: The journalist Ramita Navai
featuring in Homeland

she had heard of Zahra Kazemi, a Canadian-Iranian photojournalist who had been killed in police custody shortly before Navai had arrived in Iran.

"Every journalist knew what had happened to her and they were hinting that I would suffer the same fate. I was so petrified I started sobbing."

Navai was one of the lucky ones. A few hours after being taken, one of her journalist colleagues, Jim Muir of the BBC, noticed she was missing and started talking to the Iranians at the rally. One whispered to him that they had seen her being taken away.

"He phoned up the Ministry of Islamic Culture and Guidance and said we know you have got her, you had better release her otherwise I am going to cause a fuss about this."

Navai was released shortly afterwards.

She feels there is "no turning back" from the current protests.

"This time feels very different. I think the protests are unlike anything we have ever seen. Significantly, they span all social classes and ethnicities, and the protests have happened in every one of Iran's provinces. The protests have been a unifying force, uniting Iranians of all colours against the regime. I don't think the regime will fall imminently although I do think something has shifted and there is no going back from that. I think a very different future for Iran has now become a reality in a way that it wasn't a year ago."

She says that the protests are very localised and are happening in small towns throughout the county, not just in the big cities.

"The most organised groups seem to be the Iranian feminist and women's rights networks because they have been used to mobilising for such a long time. They are used to being arrested and imprisoned. They issue secret missives and are coordinating with some of the activists in prison."

Navai believes it is the moment for Iranian women and those of Generation Z in particular.

"The women's groups were crushed in 2009 - they were a thorn in the side of the regime. What we are seeing now is a strengthening and a rising up," she said. "In 2009, it was people my age who were and are very fearful of the regime. The younger generation - Generation Z - are absolutely fearless. My generation always felt like they had something to lose. The regime is brilliant at playing this game of giving people just enough freedom to shut them up. This younger generation have grown up in a very different world, a completely connected Iran in which

they have been influenced by global popular culture. They know what is out there in the world. They know all the opportunities that should be open and available to them and they are angry and they are fearless."

She believes a sexual awakening is also happening in Iran.

"We are talking about this being a women-led uprising, partly this is because this sexual awakening has changed the socio-cultural dynamics for Generation Z. In real terms, virginity is not the thing it used to be. So many couples are living together outside marriage that the Supreme Leader's office issued an edict saying how immoral it is. These are ordinary Iranians, not just the middle and upper class. There has been this massive socio-cultural shift. Generation Z are used to different social norms and strictures and they are not going to be told what to do. They want full autonomy not only over their bodies but over their lives."

In the fight for her own homeland, strong and fearless women will be the ones at the heart of the battle. ✖

Mark Frary is associate editor at Index

52(01):41/43|DOI:10.1177/03064220231165382

The younger generation – Generation Z – are absolutely fearless

Scope for truth

KAYA GENÇ visits a media organisation built on dissenting voices, just weeks before devastating earthquakes hit Turkey

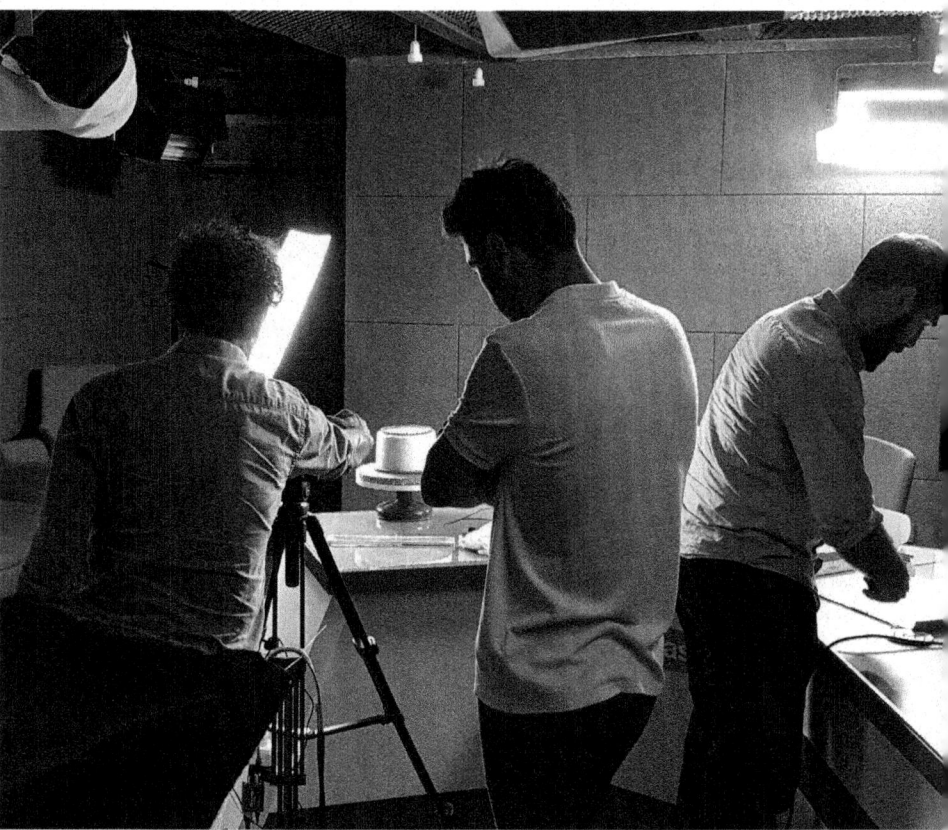

ABOVE LEFT: Staff preparing to shoot in Medyascope's new studio in Maslak, Istanbul. **ABOVE RIGHT:** Meral Akşener, leader of the opposition İYİ Party, in Medyascope's new studio in 2021

OVER THE PAST decade, Turkey's seasoned journalists have lost their jobs one after the other as cronies of the ruling AK Party complete their moves to take control of the country's mainstream media. From the Turkish editions of Vogue, GQ and CNN to once revered newspapers such as Hürriyet and Milliyet, Turkey's mainstream media has essentially become a propaganda outlet for the ruling Islamists as its most experienced reporters, editors and political commentators have been shown the door – and sometimes been condemned to "civil death" by government apparatchiks.

The audiences, it seems, have followed them out of the door as this government-controlled media has unprecedented low ratings and circulation figures. In their place, there is now a flurry of new digital journalism platforms. Media such as Medyascope, Gazete Oksijen, GAIN and FluTV now cater to millions of Turkish citizens hungry for reliable content. None of these existed a decade ago.

Nevşin Mengü, a former anchor of CNN Türk, has half a million subscribers on YouTube, and her rant on the government's U-turns over the past two decades has garnered more than 3.5 million views.

Another CNN Türk anchor, Cüneyt Özdemir (who has 1.35 million YouTube subscribers), speaks out each time a new scandal rocks the government and the mainstream media remains muted.

Özdemir's streams have broken viewing records. His live coverage of the resignation of Turkey's former finance minister – Berat Albayrak, who is President Recep Tayyip Erdogan's son-in-law – was viewed 2.5 million times. Meanwhile, Gazete Oksijen, a leftist liberal newspaper that publishes columns by sacked Turkish journalists, sells around 100,000 copies each week.

But it is Medyascope that has risen as the leading voice of a renaissance in Turkish journalism that the AK Party's ruthless assault on press freedoms ignited.

Medyascope emerged in 2015 at the newspaper office of Ruşen Çakır, a veteran journalist who started reporting in 1985. Çakır was working for a mainstream media group in 2015

when he witnessed the throttling of dissenting voices after the AK Party lost its parliamentary majority in that year's general election.

Taken off the air, Çakır increasingly felt he was persona non grata: he wasn't allowed to write, broadcast or comment. Yet the company he worked for didn't fire him, either. So he decided to use his spacious office and large salary for an experiment. One day, he placed books on top of each other on his desk and put the iPad on the top, repurposing it as his camera. Using the now defunct livestreaming app Periscope, he greeted viewers and became perhaps the first journalist to use the platform effectively in Turkey.

Over the following months, Çakır visited the weekly parliamentary meetings of opposition parties and streamed their talks on Periscope, while the network he worked for imposed a ban on all politicians not aligned with the AK Party.

CREDIT: Medyascope

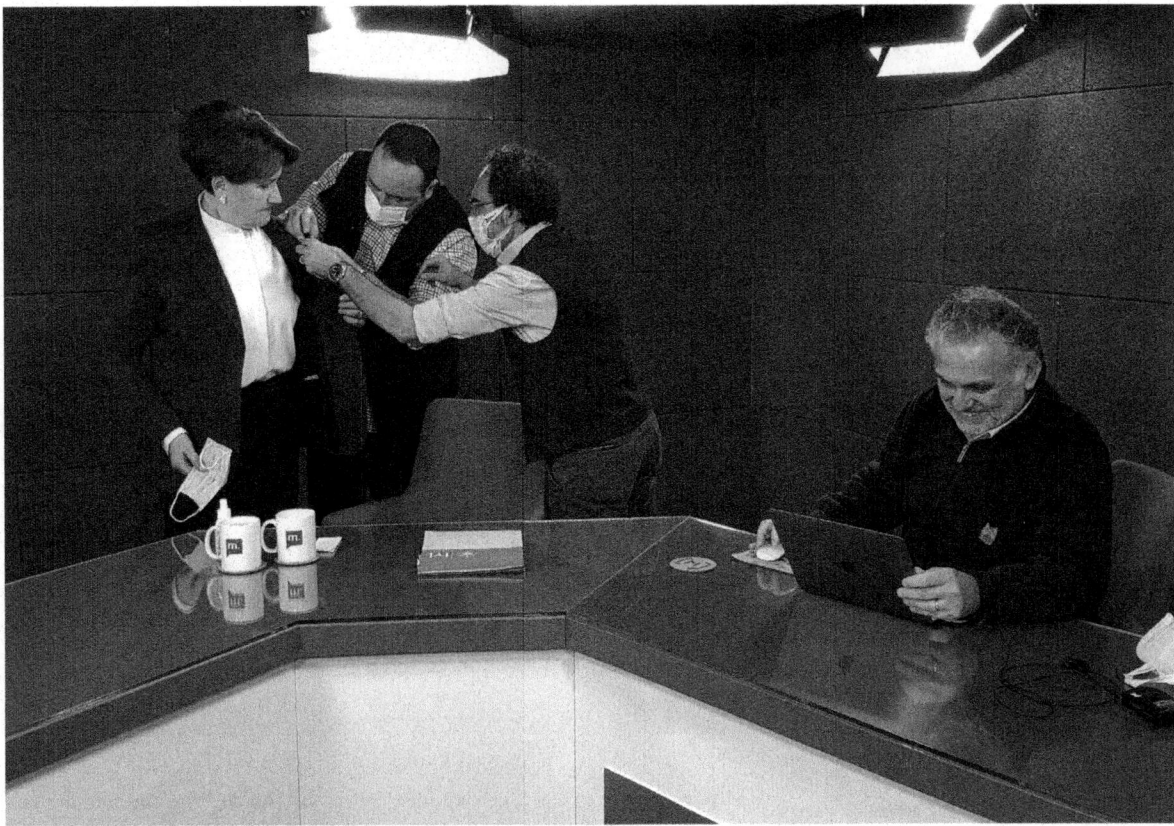

Çakır travelled through Anatolia interviewing opposition figures. In his broadcasts, he commented on the latest political developments and reached hundreds of thousands of viewers. In July 2015, an entrepreneur approached him offering to help to build a platform with a broader reach. They agreed on creating a company that would employ other journalists sacked by the Islamist regime.

Çakır's photographer friend Manuel Çıtak offered a two-floor workshop he had inherited from his family and his photography studio became Medyascope's headquarters. Young reporters got involved after emailing offering their help, Çakır used his monthly wage to invest in the studio, and soon cameras replaced iPads. Then his team came up with the name Medyascope – "a mixture of Turkish and English that reflected the platform's global ambitions" – and it launched officially on 15 August 2015.

Seasoned reporter Hıdır Göktaş

joined as its Ankara representative, opening a bureau in the Turkish capital. Representatives were appointed in Diyarbakır, Antalya, İzmir, Artvin and other Anatolian cities. Barbaros Devecioğlu, in London, became part of the team as its first foreign correspondent.

But getting funding for Medyascope proved difficult. Nobody in Turkey seemed willing to give money to a company that opposed the ruling regime. So it applied for funds from the Open Society, Chrest, Heinrich Böll and Friedrich Ebert foundations and, thanks to their support, Medyascope today employs 48 people, including technicians, reporters and editors. There are 50 freelancers producing work and dedicated podcast and social media teams. Nobody works for free.

Initially, Medyascope streamed content a few days each week. Then it began streaming each weekday. Now it streams programmes at the weekends, too. Starting at 10am and closing at

10pm, it has become indistinguishable from a television network. There are programmes on politics and shows on sports, culture and education, as well as special English-language broadcasts.

In 2016, the International Press Institute announced Medyascope would receive its 2016 Free Media Pioneer Award. In 2017, it was awarded the Reporters Without Borders Press →

ABOVE: The construction of an additional studio in Medyascope's old premises

ABOVE: A production suite in Medyascope's new studio in 2020

→ Freedom Prize. In September 2019, the Financial Times picked Medyascope for its FT Future 25: Middle East list as one of the 25 innovative start-ups from that area.

Despite its success, though, advertisers and investors in Turkey refused to support Medyascope, fearing repercussions. In 2021, its studio moved to a new building in an upper-middle-class business district of Maslak. When I paid a visit recently, Çakır and other

We're the new mainstream. We don't accept the tags of alternative, opposition or activist

Medyascope personnel were running around corridors, preparing to host interviews with several opposition leaders in the coming days.

Kaya Heyse, Medyascope's news co-ordinator, reported from Iraq and Afghanistan as a war reporter in the 1990s and worked for outlets including CNN Türk.

"There are parallels between today and the 1990s in how the media serves governmental interests, but Turkey has never had an era this authoritarian," he told Index. "This is the first time the mainstream media has been completely decimated in Turkey. Yet while the government's policies destroyed the mainstream, they also brought a solution in the form of institutions like Medyascope."

Medyascope's policy, Heyse said, is to be pluralist and leave no political view uncovered. He emphasised that Medyascope was not an opposition platform. "We're not activists. We're just journalists," he said. "We're the new mainstream. We don't accept the tags of alternative, opposition or activist media."

Aside from funding difficulties, Medyascope faced two significant backlashes. First, its website became unreachable for 17 hours the day after the attempted coup on 15 July 2016. Then, in the summer of 2021, the government began using the term "foreign-funded media" to discredit Medyascope, accusing it of being a nefarious tool of Western democracies against Turkey.

"We thought these coordinated attacks would go away in two days," Heyse recalled. "They didn't."

It was decided that the best course was to continue to do their job correctly.

"In authoritarian systems, they may close down your institution and detain you. But we believed that as long as you do journalism properly, nothing would happen," he said.

Over the weeks following February's earthquakes, Medyascope journalists offered a window into the earthquake

RIGHT: Staff gathered in Medyascope's old newsroom

zone, even as other journalists were arrested for their reporting. In the village of Söğütlü, Medyascope reported that "Citizens died waiting because no help came", and produced a special broadcast discussing the responsibilities of the administration.

Medyascope's peak moment, in terms of its popularity, came after the 2019 local elections – between March 2019, when the opposition won and the AK Party annulled the results of the election (accusing Istanbul's progressive mayor of being a "thief" and a "terrorist"), and the re-elections in June 2019, when the opposition candidate won with a massive margin.

"We had incredible numbers in those days with a limited staff," said Heyse, recalling a real sense of satisfaction at a job done well. A recent Medyascope exposé about child brides in İsmailağa, a government-supported Islamic sect, broke viewing records, and they have ambitious plans for the upcoming elections.

But does he expect trouble on election night, as many do? "I'm optimistic. I think Turkey has still not turned into a Russia or an Azerbaijan—even if there's potential for that," he said. If the AK Party falls into opposition, he added, Medyascope would open its doors to its members for interviews.

"We'd welcome Erdogan, too, of course, but he should be willing to let us interview him properly," said Heyse. "It won't be like a CNN Türk show where the anchor says: 'Sir, speak. We're listening to whatever you want to tell us.'"

As for Çakır, the platform's founder, Medyascope's success story is enough reason to be optimistic about Turkey. He told Index: "In a country that is utterly polarised, where there are multiple assaults on the freedom of the press, we've set out to create a platform for free, original and independent journalism that refuses to polarise. We did so by trying to weave traditional journalism with new technologies. We largely succeeded, thanks to contributions from so many people from Turkey and abroad, and with a crew made mostly of young, female journalists.

"We've come much further than we imagined when we set out. This makes me happy. We were realistic, and we demanded the impossible. We saw and showed others a platform like Medyascope wasn't impossible in the first place." ✖

Kaya Genç is Turkey's contributing editor for Index. He is based in Istanbul

52(01):44/47|DOI:10.1177/03064220231165383

Medyascope at a glance

44
The staff members keeping Medyascope running

The homes of Medyascope content — including an app launched in 2021 and five separate YouTube channels

50
The approximate number of contributors

25+
The reach, in millions, each month

Medyascope's website plays host to this many million visitors

1,000 News pieces penned for the website every month

500
Monthly videos shot, packaged and delivered

Data provided by Medyascope in January 2022

Ukraine's media battleground

EMILY COUCH provides two powerful examples of how fraught reporting on this country under siege has become

PICTURED: Ukrainian
President Volodymyr
Zelensky at his first
news conference since
the 2022 war began

I N A TIME of war, all bets are off. Society exists in a protracted state of exception and political norms often go out of the window. The situation in Ukraine, now entering the 12th month of its fight for survival against Russia, is no different. Nonetheless, to borrow Carl von Clausewitz's oft-quoted maxim, war – while apparently exceptional – is the continuation of politics by other means. Politics continues as bombs fall, so attention is on a new media law in Ukraine, with questions about whether it respects human rights.

"The war has made everything complicated, and in terms of human rights it has certainly thrown us back by some 10 years, including the situation with freedom of the press," said Iryna Matviyishyn, a journalist

with the Kyiv Independent.

She spoke to Index about Law No 2,693, simply named On Media. It came into force after being signed by President Volodymyr Zelensky on 29 December last year. The law underwent several revisions but its core principles remained the same: centralising existing media laws, establishing a regulatory framework for mass and online media, and curbing Russian disinformation.

While the law was given the green light by the EU – which granted Ukraine candidate status in June 2022 – it leaves many journalists and free expression advocates uneasy. Chief among their concerns are the lack of transparency in the review process and the comprehensive powers granted to the state broadcasting regulator, including

the ability to shut down without a court ruling news sites that are not officially registered as media. According to the Institute of Mass Information, a Ukrainian NGO that focuses on media freedom, the regulator is unlikely to be truly independent. Its members will be appointed by Zelensky and Ukraine's parliament, the Verkhovna Rada, where his party has an absolute majority.

Since assuming office in April 2019, Zelensky has had a prickly relationship with the press. In 2021, editor-in-chief of **Censor.net** Yurii Butusov faced a criminal investigation into a video on his social media. Butusov claimed that the investigation was retaliation for his widely publicised criticism of Zelensky.

As of 2 January this year, 6,919 Ukrainian civilians, many of them children, have lost their lives to Russian attacks and 11,075 more have suffered injuries, according to the UN. But amidst these horrors, the issue of media freedom persists.

Nationwide martial law has led to significant restrictions. In April 2022, the Verkhovna Rada passed bill No 7,214, establishing criminal liability for any media outlet deemed to be distributing propaganda from the "Russian neo-Nazi totalitarian regime". This included using the Z and V symbols.

The new legislation also empowered the commander-in-chief of the armed forces of Ukraine to establish an accreditation procedure for media representatives and their admission to military facilities. In general, Matviyishyn said, Ukrainian journalists "understand [the necessity of] the regulations", even if it makes their work more difficult.

Ihor Rozkladai, deputy director of the Centre for Democracy and Rule of Law, a Ukrainian NGO that helped draft the media law, shares this understanding.

"We can talk about freedoms after the war," he said. The current focus, he added, should be on the crimes against journalists perpetrated by Russian forces. As for the review process preceding the law's adoption, Rozkladai said: "I have worked with legislation for many, many years and I can say that if you have a working group of more than 10 people it becomes absolutely ineffective [...] Transparency for transparency's sake without efficacy? No, I do not want to play such games."

Ukraine's president has garnered accolades such as Time Magazine's coveted Person of the Year title. But while an unscrupulous leader might see this acclaim as a carte blanche to push through legislation that tightens his grip on power, Rozkladai dismisses this possibility.

"Every politician of reasonable intelligence understands that to pressure the media in Ukraine is a very bad idea. If you start pressuring the media, you will have Maidan," he said, referring

to the mass protests that took place in Kyiv's central square in 2004 and again in 2013 and 2014.

Matviyishyn claimed that the authorities did take much of the criticism from civil society into account when pushing through the bill, but said: "We'll see how it will work because, in Ukraine, often something is written but it is applied in a different way, and often [the authorities] find loopholes."

There might be doubts around the review process and provisions of Ukraine's media law but, as Matviyishyn's comments show, to many people they pale in comparison with the crimes perpetrated by Russian forces against media workers.

Matviyishyn, too, highlighted the danger of foreigners failing to listen, recalling her work with US journalists from NPR in the first three months of the war.

"There were quite a few cases when they didn't understand why you shouldn't look for a strategic facility (like a storage of wheat) when Russia was targeting them. Nonetheless, they kept asking civilians where it was after Ukrainian officials refused to talk."

Ukrainian journalists are under no illusions regarding the restrictions or the potential of the state to abuse the media law's provisions. Civil society continues to provide essential oversight of domestic policy, even if the focus is now on Russia's attacks on Ukrainian media workers. Ukraine is fighting for its existence as a democratic state. The success of this will determine the fate of the country's media for decades to come.

The language of allies
The scandal surrounding Amnesty International's August 2022 report on the tactics of the Ukrainian military illustrates what can happen if international organisations do not respond sensitively to alleged violations by Ukraine. In the report, Amnesty claimed that Ukrainian forces were "endangering civilians" by operating

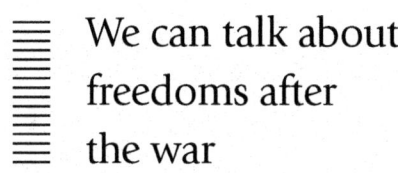

We can talk about freedoms after the war

weapons from, and setting up bases in, populated residential areas.

Outrage ensued, with the head of Amnesty's Ukraine office resigning in protest, accusing the organisation of spreading Russian propaganda. The report was enthusiastically taken up by Russia. Its UK embassy shared the report on Twitter with the hashtag "#StopNaziUkraine".

Since last year's invasion, Ukrainians have been vocal both on and offline about the West's tendency to dismiss their perspectives. "Listen to Ukrainians. Amplify them. Share the stories," tweeted bestselling Ukrainian-US author Tetyana Denford.

In the Facebook post in which she announced her resignation, Amnesty's Ukraine field office Oksana Pokalchuk decried the organisation's leadership as "deaf" to the pain experienced by Ukrainians. She stated that those who are safely out of harm's way must take account of local contexts.

"I am convinced that our research should be done scrupulously and with people in mind, whose lives often directly depend on the words and actions of international organisations," she wrote.

As the insights from journalists and human rights defenders such as Matviyishyn and Rozkladai demonstrate, heeding the warning of Amnesty's example does not mean letting democratic principles fall by the wayside. Rather, international human rights advocates are finding the balance between upholding media freedoms and remaining sensitive to realities on the ground. ✖

Emily Couch is contributing editor (Ukraine and Russia) of Index on Censorship

52(01):48/49|DOI:10.1177/03064220231165384

Storytime is dragged into the guns row

Relaxed gun laws and the rise of anti-LGBTQ+ sentiment is silencing minority communities in the USA. **FRANCIS CLARKE** speaks to some of those affected

AS SCHOOL MANAGER at Red Oak Community School in Columbus, Ohio, it is in Cheryl Ryan's nature to be smiley and chatty, as she is when I talk to her over Zoom one day in February. But in early December 2022, as her name appeared on national news sites across the USA, she struggled to maintain her cheery demeanour. Ryan was organising a Drag Queen Story Hour event at the First Unitarian Universalist Church of Columbus, which runs the school. It was meant to be a festive school fundraiser. A reading of children's books by drag performers attended by children and their families, it's an event she had previously held successfully. This time was different. It caught the attention of the Proud Boys and Patriot Front, US neo-fascist groups that engage in political violence.

"In the past we had no pushback, but around May or June, Proud Boys started tracking these events. They started to make it part of their thing, which I wasn't aware of," Ryan said.

Despite being held around the world since 2015, Drag Queen Story Hour events in the USA became a focus for far-right groups in 2022. The hosts and attendees have received threats and protests, although most events have still

gone ahead. Ryan's did not. A mix-up meant no security would be present and it was simply too dangerous to proceed. Hers was the first Drag Queen Story Hour cancelled last minute in the USA.

"We knew they would come armed with semi-automatic weapons, and we didn't know how many armed counter-protesters might show up as well," she said. "Anybody could show up openly bearing guns, which is the ridiculous place that our gun laws are in here. Being allowed to 'open carry' in that way with automatic rifles is insane."

The issue of whether a state is "open carry" – meaning having the right to carry a gun both publicly and openly – is having a detrimental effect on the sorts of events that are programmed in the USA. This, when coupled with a rise in anti-LGBTQ+ sentiment, is a toxic mix. At a Drag Queen Story Hour held in a Nevada library in June 2022, an armed right-wing extremist reportedly tried to enter a library to intimidate attendees. At another held in an Oregon pub in October 2022, around 200 demonstrators and counter-demonstrators – some of them armed – faced off outside the venue.

Giffords Law Center, which campaigns for stronger gun laws across the USA, says more than 30 states allow the general open carry of a handgun without any licence or permit. This rises to more than 40 states for long guns.

Adam Winkler is a professor at the UCLA School of Law and a specialist in US constitutional law and gun policy. Referencing divisive views, he said: "There is an increasing movement by gun advocates to appear at protests with guns, and where it's lawful it's seen that the presence of a gun is not indicative of a hostile or intimidating act.

Anybody could show up openly bearing guns

"However, it's easy to see how protesters feel the presence of guns is intimidating, and I agree that bringing guns to protests does have a chilling effect on the speech and expression of others."

When asked about potential future change for open-carry guns, Winkler said he believed the laws were loosening, not tightening. "As long as they aren't used in an exclusively and overtly intimidating fashion, we're likely to see the Supreme Court one day say guns are a protected form of speech. America is changing, but not in the way some people might hope."

While acknowledging guns can be used to intimidate, Winkler said they have also been used as a form of protest themselves. He explained: "People might think of the Black Panthers with firearms outside state legislators to protest laws designed to disarm them. We now know

LEFT: Rich Kuntz, also known as Gidget, reads to children during a Drag Queen Story Hour in 2019 in Orlando

Hunt's comments come as several states consider legislative proposals to ban children from attending any sort of drag-related event. In June 2022, Texas state representative Bryan Slaton said a law was necessary to protect children from "perverted adults", while in the same month Florida governor Ron DeSantis announced he would consider a proposal to ban minors from drag events. In October 2022, more than 30 Republicans in the House of Representatives signed a bill to prohibit federal money from being used to make "sexually oriented" materials available to children under the age of 10, which would include Drag Queen Story Hour events. Hunt feels the legislation is being used as an attack on freedom of expression.

"Broadly worded bills go after these events, trying to take away a parental choice whether to have their kids attend, and it's a broader attack on the LGBTQ+ community. They are designed to create fear about the community across our country," she said.

Cheryl Ryan agrees, explaining that politicians "get a wedge social issue and get everybody to pick it up the way they want. They're just laser-focused on the LGBTQ+ community". She said: "I think there are eight states trying to outlaw drag shows altogether or [have them] listed as porn. They are trying to point everybody in this direction."

Ryan says her decision to cancel her event was also influenced by the deadly mass shooting at an LGBTQ+ nightclub in Colorado Springs a few weeks earlier, as it made "the danger and the risk more real".

"I think for the LGBTQ+ community, that's not new for them," she said. "Sadly, there is always something that could happen." ✖

Francis Clarke is editorial assistant at Index

there was never intent to cause havoc, take hostages or use those firearms, but [they were] meant as a potent symbol of autonomy and self-defence."

Drag Queen Story Hour, however, is an event for children led by a drag performer – a member of a minority community that has increasingly been a focus of protests in general, including from the far-right.

Glaad, the world's largest LGBTQ+ advocacy organisation, reported that in 2022, drag events faced at least 141 protests and significant threats, including armed protests both at Drag Queen Story Hours and, more broadly, at drag shows, bingos and brunches.

The Armed Conflict Location and Event Data Project (ACLED) said that far-right militant movements such as the Proud Boys and Patriot Front upped their engagement in anti-LGBTQ+

demonstrations from 16 events in 2021 to 52 as of mid-November 2022. While ACLED doesn't provide information on armed protests, it says that protests are four times more likely to turn violent if far-right militants are involved.

Olivia Hunt, policy director for the National Centre for Transgender Equality, told Index: "There's a clear line between politicians using anti-queer rhetoric to drum up their base, leading to social media accounts picking that up and creating a moral panic, to instances of threats and acts of violence.

"Last year, there were at least 145 attacks or intimidation tactics used against family-friendly drag events. They have generally characterised any drag performances as sexually motivated, and people will worry about staging Drag Queen Story Hours for the risk of violence."

52(01):50/51|DOI:10.1177/03064220231165386

Those we must not leave behind

The UK government has failed in its task to rescue Afghans. **MARTIN BRIGHT** speaks to members of a new Index network aiming to help those whose lives are in imminent danger

ALI BEHZAD FIRST contacted Index in September 2021. He was writing from Kabul, where the Taliban had been in power for a month, and he was desperate. He had been working for a refugee news agency and Tamadon TV, a station that broadcast to the minority Shia population of Afghanistan. With the arrival of the new regime, he faced a bleak future.

His message was grim: "I have opted to approach you in order to seek protection from security threats against me. By consideration of increasing danger and as the result of death threats that I have received, my life is in jeopardy."

He explained he was in danger because of his journalism and human rights activism, but also because he was from the minority Hazara community, which was facing a potential genocide by the incoming regime. In his email, Behzad called for solidarity from those who, like him, "seek the truth and advocate for free speech".

In the early weeks of the Taliban takeover – in common with many other free expression, human rights and media organisations – Index was

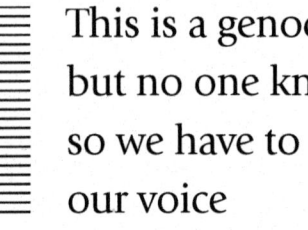

This is a genocide, but no one knows, so we have to raise our voice

deluged by requests for help from journalists-at-risk who were trapped in Afghanistan. Behzad and his fellow journalists were part of an organisation called Afghan Journalists Trend (AJT) and they soon compiled a list of around 300 of their colleagues they claimed needed immediate assistance to leave the country.

Index initially set up a small support group on the secure messaging app Signal to help co-ordinate support, though we explained that we were in no position to exfiltrate people from the country.

Verification was a serious problem. An open letter from AJT published by the Association of European Journalists (AEJ) in October 2021 claimed that wealthy individuals in Afghanistan were posing as journalists while genuine reporters were being left behind. "This is great persecution for Afghanistan's well-known journalists, who have spent many years in the most difficult of conditions, feeling responsible for their country and its people, for institutionalising freedom of expression," it said.

Even organisations which specialised in working directly with journalists-at-risk, such as Reporters Without Borders (RSF) and PEN International, were struggling with the sheer volume of requests for help.

Another problem was the risk of raising false hope. After the initial evacuation mission, it became increasingly clear that it was near impossible for Afghan journalists to get out of the country, and press freedom

organisations were forced to send out standard email responses directing people to international humanitarian assistance programmes.

To this day, the advice from RSF, one of the most effective organisations during this crisis, is stark: "Unfortunately, the needs of Afghan journalists far outweigh the international assistance programmes currently available… We regret that because of the incredibly high number of assistance requests from Afghanistan, our team cannot offer individual consultations. Inquiries via email, phone, social media channels or Messenger will NOT be answered. Requests or documents that you email to RSF will not be processed."

And yet, thanks to the efforts of some committed individuals and dedicated organisations, a handful of journalists have managed to get out of Afghanistan – mainly to Germany and Canada, as well as to Spain, France and Kosovo.

Ali Behzad is one of them. The AEJ took up his case and worked closely with the Agency for International Co-operation (GIZ), an NGO based in Bonn and sponsored by the German Ministry for Economic Development. In August 2022, almost exactly a year after the Taliban takeover of Kabul, he and his wife – a TV camerawoman – and his two small children were relocated to Bavaria via Pakistan. Since arriving in Germany, his wife has given birth to a daughter.

Behzad spoke to Index from his new home near Schweinfurt, where he and his family are living in a castle as guests of the German government. He knows it will not be easy finding work in Germany – although he has already begun taking intensive German lessons – and he has no illusions about what he has left behind.

"The situation has not changed. The Taliban didn't change," he said. "They are not allowing journalists, especially women journalists, to work, and any output is censored by the Taliban. Most people lost their jobs and cannot support their families."

ABOVE: Afghan-Canadian journalist Zahra Nader, editor-in-chief of Zan Times, which covers human rights violations in Afghanistan, speaks at the Women, Peace and Security - UN Security Council Open Debate in October 2022

Sparked by his story, we decided to reactivate Index's Signal support group and find out what had happened to the other members. The stories could not be more contrasting.

Freshta Hemmati, a young female journalist not long out of university, had just received news that she had won a scholarship for a master's degree in Astana, Kazakhstan, when the Taliban swept into Kabul. Aged just 25, she seized an opportunity to leave the country, but it meant leaving her family behind. While in Astana, she wrote her thesis comparing the situation for women journalists during two decades of democracy with life under the Taliban. In 2022, she was granted asylum in Canada and now works as the CEO of the Afghan Journalists Support Organisation to help colleagues still at risk and alert the world to the deteriorating situation.

"If we don't get the international community united over this, we will not be able to stand against terrorism. This is a genocide, but no one knows, so we have to raise our voice. There is lots of condemnation, but no action. Just do something."

While Hemmati and Behzad are

building new lives in exile, others have not been so fortunate. Hasib (not his real name) was working for a scientific publication that also promoted the rights of women prior to August 2021. The arrival of the Taliban meant he immediately lost his job and he is now in hiding from the authorities. He told Index: "In order to continue living, and because of threats against journalists, I buy and collect old iron, plastic and used water and Pepsi bottles in the back alleys of Kabul and sell them again." He has applied to evacuation schemes with various Western institutions, but with no success.

One female TV presenter in the group, a familiar face on Afghan TV, was determined to stay and fight for the rights of women journalists. In the autumn of 2021, Saira sent us regular footage of demonstrations against the regime, with protesters demanding that women be permitted to go to school and university and not banned from the workplace. By February 2023, the tone of her messages had changed. "I can't work," she said. "The restrictions for us ladies are increasing every day. Afghanistan has no future. There is a lot of oppression." A sad face emoji followed and then three simple words: "I lost hope." Publishing her real name would put her life at risk.

Even for journalists who have escaped to neighbouring countries, the situation can be perilous. In January, we were contacted by another female news anchor, Mahtab, who had fled to Islamabad in October 2021.

She wrote: "During this period, I have gone through hell – Pakistan is little different to Afghanistan. Here, too, there are Taliban sympathisers. There is no safety, no job opportunities, inflation is high. There is much discrimination, racism and prejudice in the society and there is hostility towards Afghan people in general – and women in particular."

A month later, we heard from a reporter and women's rights activist who had also fled to Pakistan, where

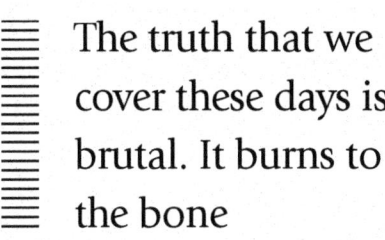

The truth that we cover these days is brutal. It burns to the bone

she was living in destitution with a tiny baby. As a journalist she had covered Taliban war crimes and violations of women's rights, and as a women's rights activist she had publicly criticised the Taliban on public platforms. After a series of death threats, Sahar had no option other than fleeing Kabul. She told us: "Now it's more than one year that I'm without any work and any income with my five-month-old baby boy. My economic situation is too bad, I really need your help and kindness."

Around the time we heard from Mahtab and Sahar, we also received news from the Afghan Journalists Support Organisation that the Pakistani authorities had arrested a number of Afghan journalists in Islamabad. Although they were later released, there remains a concern that exiles may face deportation back to Kabul when their visas expire. The very fact that they have left the country would put them at risk on their return.

Meanwhile, in Afghanistan, the crackdown on independent news outlets continues. In February, the Committee to Protect Journalists reported that the Taliban was restricting Afghan access to Voice of America and Radio Free Europe/Radio Liberty. In the same month, Tamadon TV – where Behzad used to work – was raided by armed men who beat reporters and security staff. Taliban officials in Helmand province also banned all media outlets from distributing videos and photographs, and independent media in Parwan province was ordered to fall in line with the Taliban's Bakhtar News Agency.

The Nai-Supporting Open Media in Afghanistan, a free expression NGO, →

PICTURED: An exiled
Afghan journalist,
Elyaas Ehsas, at an
apartment in Paris on
17 September 2021

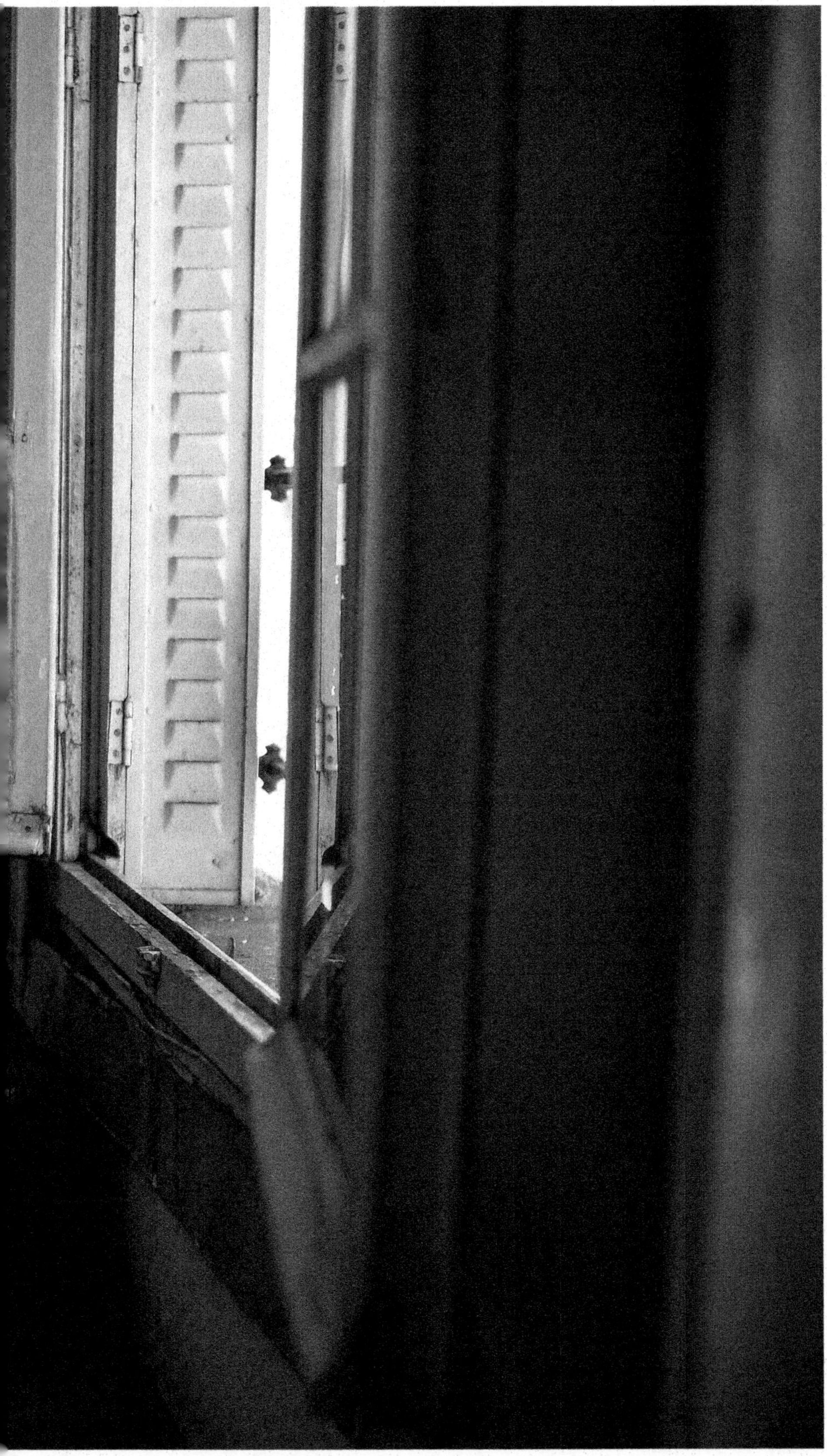

→ has reported that half of all radio stations in the country have closed. The outlook is grim for anyone who cares about a free media for Afghanistan, and especially so for women. RSF has reported that 84% of women journalists have lost their jobs and that there could be as few as 39 journalists in total now working in Kabul.

But all is not yet completely lost. Salma Niazi, who fled Afghanistan last year, set up The Afghan Times in September 2022 in Islamabad, using her personal savings. She runs a team of five female journalists, writing in Pashtun and English, three of whom are still working undercover in Afghanistan. Recent stories included a report on the arrest of women's

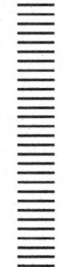

> The outlook is grim for anyone who cares about a free media for Afghanistan

rights activist Narges Sadat in Kabul, a feature on child marriage and a news story about the mental health problems among female students unable to attend university.

Another, Rukhshana Media, was set up in November 2020 by Hazara journalist Zahra Joya, who now runs the organisation from exile in London. Rukhshana Media received the Marie Colvin Award at the British Journalism Awards in 2021 and Joya was named as one of Time's 12 Women of the Year in 2022.

Writing in Index just after the fall of Kabul, Joya's colleague Zahra Nader spoke of her nightmare watching the events of 15 August unfold, but also of her determination to report "what →

CREDIT: Christophe Archambault/AFP/Getty

If the Taliban caught them then they would be tortured, imprisoned

→ women have lost – and what they continue to lose – as the new regime expands its power".

She has been as good as her word. Based in Toronto, Nader set up her own publication, Zan Times, in August 2022 to report on human rights in Afghanistan. Speaking at a recent Canadian Journalists for Free Expression gala, where she received the Kathy Gannon Legacy Award from the Coalition for Women in Journalism, she said: "The truth that we cover these days is brutal. It burns to the bone. It traumatises you. It is a nightmare that haunts us even in daylight. Yet some refuse to accept loss at the hands of the Taliban."

She went on to pay tribute to her female colleagues on the ground in Afghanistan, saying: "They endure the brutal and traumatising reality of life under Taliban rule, knowing that if the Taliban caught them then they would be tortured, imprisoned, and god knows what would happen to them."

Since the Taliban entered Kabul, Index has been campaigning for safe passage of Afghan writers and artists. In September 2021, we organised an open letter to The Times with our friends from Good Chance Theatre to urge the UK government to provide refuge for those under direct threat. This plea was signed by more than 80 prominent figures from the arts and media.

The letter recognised that the past two decades had been a golden age of creativity in Afghanistan and a period of political dissent and relative freedom for the media. "With the Taliban takeover

'I have gone through hell'

One female Afghan journalist, Mahtab Bibi, shares her shocking story of fleeing Afghanistan and what came after

I AM A young Afghan broadcast journalist with almost five years of experience in the field. I have worked as a news anchor, presenter and reporter during the course of my career, and have been associated with a number of renowned media organisations in Afghanistan.

Due to my work, I have confronted many threats from house raids, online bullying, digital and cyber-attacks, and harassment. I had received several threats from the Taliban before their rise to power. My Facebook account was hacked twice. I had to change my mobile number multiple times as a result.

After the takeover of Kabul, the Taliban launched a crackdown on the media and raids on the houses of the journalists started. Understanding the severity of the situation I tried to flee the country multiple times, but due to closure of borders I didn't succeed. I had to go into hiding and luckily I narrowly escaped a day before the raid of my house. I travelled with my elder brother to a location in the north-east of the country where I stayed for a month and a half with some distant relatives before fleeing clandestinely to Pakistan after borders were opened in October 2021.

Since then, I have been living alone in Pakistan, away from my family and loved ones, with no job and livelihood. I have faced and I am still facing a plethora of issues here in Pakistan.

I have been forced to live in unhygienic slums due to financial issues. I have spent many days without food and when I do eat, it is often just once a day. I have been ill many times, but I haven't been to hospital

or received any medication, and have been suffering from mental health issues like anxiety, depression, insomnia and stress. I haven't been able to purchase clothes for myself since I fled Afghanistan.

I have also been a victim of discrimination and racism due to my ethnicity, nationality and religion. I was kicked out of two dormitories due to my nationality and ethnicity and also faced harassment and discrimination. In two places I have stayed my money was taken as a deposit before allowing me to live in the apartment as a tenant, but in both of these places my money was not returned when leaving.

I have struggled to meet even my most basic needs, but support from Reporters Without Borders and Frontline Defenders has given me some respite and these funds have enabled me to survive.

During this period, I have gone through hell – Pakistan is little different to Afghanistan. Here too there are Taliban sympathisers. There is no safety, no job opportunities, inflation is high. There is much discrimination, racism and prejudice in the society and there is hostility towards Afghan people in general and women in particular.

A particularly unpleasant incident happened some months ago. One evening in July last year I was assaulted by an unknown biker while returning from the supermarket. The biker grabbed me and groped my body and was trying to pull me down to sexually assault me. But luckily this happened in the street near my flat, where I shouted loudly

of the country, this rich legacy is in imminent peril," the letter stated. "We now have a duty to those artists, writers and film-makers who will be silenced if we do not act immediately."

At the time, it was felt that simply offering refuge would not be enough, and the letter went on: "We also call on those in positions of influence in the creative industries to help those who have escaped to continue their vital work and safeguard the culture of

Afghanistan for future generations."

Little did those signing the letter know that so few journalists, let alone writers and artists, would find refuge in the UK. And that's despite the UK government pledging that they would.

Under the Afghan Citizens Resettlement Scheme, announced by Prime Minister Boris Johnson in August 2021, the UK government committed itself to resettling up to 20,000 people at risk. A priority was given to those who and, after a lot of pushing and shoving, I was able to escape. Since this incident I have been too scared to go out, even during the day. Harassment in the streets for women is very normal here. I have to endure shameful touching, gazes and catcalls in public when I go out for anything and unfortunately, being Afghan, we can't do anything about it.

Now my situation is getting worse due to the long wait to relocate to a safe country. Moreover, the Pakistani authorities have put more restrictions on visas for Afghani people, as the majority of visas are either denied or there are long delays. There is a clear reluctance from the government to issue visas to Afghans. I was on a one-year visa to Pakistan which expired August 2022. I applied for a visa extension in June 2022 but I have not received a decision yet. If the visa request is rejected I will be liable to pay heavy fines ($500) and face other legal liabilities. In December, the Pakistani authorities announced that any Afghan without a valid visa would be arrested and put into prison for three years or deported back to Afghanistan.

I know of one Afghani family who were put in jail by the Pakistani authorities due to illegal overstay. The male guardian of the family died in the jail. The rest of the family is still in jail. We all are really scared and fearful about this matter because we can't afford any legal and financial liability or penalty. We also can't go back to our country due to the severity of the threats

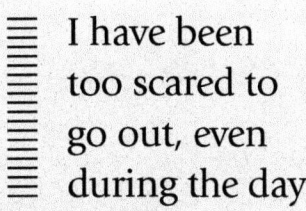

I have been too scared to go out, even during the day

to our life and safety and a really uncertain and dark future for women.

I am asking for assistance in relocating to any safe country where I can continue my journalism safely, complete my education and support myself and my family. In addition to serious threats for my life there is no future back home for women right now. There is a ban on education for women, a ban on women working in the media and NGOs and a ban on free movement of women outside without the veil and a male guardian. As a human being I deserve the right to life, safety, education and work. I deserve freedom of movement and freedom of expression.. I am desperately and anxiously looking for any help in this regard and assistance with the financial support to meet my immediate and basic needs.

I hope my plea will be heard and heeded in the right corners and a hand of support will be extended.

Mahtab Bibi is a journalist from Afghanistan. This article is an edited version of one which appeared online. It is similar in its description to many we receive today

Until the UK government gets its act together, they will continue to suffer a half-life of fear and desperation

stood up for the values of democracy, women's rights, freedom of speech and the rule of law – including a specific reference to journalists. The scheme was formally opened in January 2022 and was initially designed for those who were evacuated in 2021. A second "pathway" was opened in June 2022 for those who had escaped to neighbouring countries. A third pathway is planned to open fully this year.

Index, RSF, PEN and the National

Union of Journalists have urged ministers to clarify how the scheme will help journalists-at-risk and have offered their assistance in referring and verifying journalists hoping to come to the UK.

We now know that RSF has succeeded in helping more than 200 journalists to leave Afghanistan. The German government announced a federal assistance programme in October 2022, which has already been swamped with applications. Even tiny Kosovo has a scheme to help journalists-at risk in collaboration with the European Federation of Journalists and the European Centre for Press and Media Freedom. It is not known how many journalists have reached the UK's shores, but it is not likely to be more than a handful as most international media support organisations have given up on the country as a viable option.

The failure to live up to their pledge is not lost on those such as Hemmati and Niazi, impatient to support Afghan journalists on the ground. Both told Index they did not understand the UK government's attitude. "We are... shocked that the UK government has not yet fulfilled its promises," said Niazi.

The UK parades its proud history of welcoming dissident writers from authoritarian regimes. Indeed, this magazine is founded on that tradition. But that history appears to have stalled when it comes to Afghanistan. There is little doubt that when Ali Behzad learns the language, he will make an important contribution to Germany. Canada is already rightly proud of Freshta Hemmati and Zahra Nader.

What of Hasib and Saira, Mahtab and Sahar? Until the UK government gets its act together, they will continue to suffer a half-life of fear and desperation. And we will never know what they might have brought to the intellectual life of this country. ✖

Martin Bright is editor-at-large at Index

52(01):52/57|DOI:10.1177/03064220231165387

SPECIAL REPORT

"Not all commit obvious crimes against women but they endorse the
foot soldiers who do the dirty work of upholding the patriarchy"

ANINDITA GHOSE | UNCLE IS WATCHING | P.82

Modi's singular vision for India

India used to be a country for everyone. Now it's only for Hindus – and uncritical ones at that, **SALIL TRIPATHI** writes

ABOVE: Indian Prime Minister Narendra Modi during the Independence Day celebrations at the historic Red Fort in Delhi, August 2022

NDIA CELEBRATED ITS 75th anniversary as an independent nation last year. It also overtook its former colonial ruler, Great Britain, in terms of the size of its economy – gate-crashing into the league as the world's fifth-largest. This year, it will host the G20 Summit, a global gathering of major international economies. And next year, when Indians vote in the general election, they will break their own record of participating in the world's largest exercise of expression of democratic franchise. With 1.4 billion people, India has the world's largest electorate, with some three-quarters of the population – those aged 18 or older – having the right to vote.

And yet this is a country where journalists are being jailed; where the courts have complied with the demands of the executive; where the media ask "How high?" when the government asks journalists to jump; where minorities face significant discrimination; and where those who dissent or question the state must prepare themselves for prosecutorial procedures that can keep them entangled for decades.

India was always a flawed democracy. During the years when Jawaharlal Nehru was the prime minister (1947-64) the rebel poet Majrooh Sultanpuri was jailed briefly for his tempestuous poem which was critical of him. During the Emergency, when Nehru's daughter Indira Gandhi was prime minister, press freedom was suppressed and some journalists went to jail. In the 1980s, the government attempted to pass a severe law criminalising defamation, but backtracked when journalists opposed it.

The India of 2023 is fundamentally

different from what the platitudes suggest. While it is the world's most populous democracy holding elections, it is not the largest democracy. It has the structures of a democracy but it has weakened democracy's functions. It has a parliament where the opposition is powerless. It has a judiciary, but its courts delay judgments on crucial issues, making them pointless, or cast them aside as if they were irrelevant. And it has a media – not state-owned – which is now eager to demonstrate how nationalistic and patriotic it is and to curry favour with the ruling party.

Under its hugely popular and charismatic leader Narendra Modi, India has become a different country. Modi is not to be revered as a democrat but feared as what can happen in a society that has lost its moorings along with its values. Like Rodrigo Duterte, the former president of the Philippines, he can be uncouth; unlike him, he knows who not to offend. Like Turkish president Recep Tayyip Erdogan, he knows how to bully his own people; unlike him, he is not part of an alliance such as Nato that forces him to take a position. Like Viktor Orbán, the prime minister of Hungary, he is bigoted; unlike him, he does not have to reckon with an imperial power threatening him with potential subjugation. He is a strongman who has risen to power because he made the privileged majority – Hindus – falsely believe that they were persecuted, and he has presented himself as their saviour. And far too many believe in him and in his rhetoric. It will be a shock if he does not win in 2024.

This would have been something only India – and Indians – might have worried about if it were a matter concerning a nation of little consequence. But by later this year, India will be the world's most populous country. Ideally, the world's most populous country would be a genuine democracy – a strong counter to the rise of authoritarian China. But it is not.

As mentioned, India has always had

The world is riled about what happens in China, for example, but it gives India a free pass

human rights violations – its Partition in 1947 spawned mass violence in which hundreds of thousands of people died in Punjab and Bengal, and people carry memories of those scars, influencing their choices. But the genius of Mahatma Gandhi's non-violence and Nehru's inclusiveness was that those men succeeded in convincing India that it was a great project; an idea larger than itself, where it didn't matter what your sex was, what your language was, what your caste was, or, most importantly, what your faith was, as long as you said you belonged to India. That was the initial conceit – what Salman Rushdie once called "the dream we had all agreed to dream".

The flawed India of the past also had corrective mechanisms. At its most extreme, Indira Gandhi was voted out in 1977. More broadly, in its 75 years it has voted out governments in seven of the 17 elections it has held – a record for which the people should justly feel proud. In the past, its courts have taken measly postcards from the poor and treated those as writ petitions, forcing the government to act, and its independent media has been a watchdog which growled and barked at those corrupt in power. That was until 2014 when Modi took office.

India is falling in the UN's human development indicators; Freedom House no longer considers India as "free"; and it is the only "nominal democracy" among the top 10 countries that jails writers, according to PEN America. Reporters Sans Frontieres says more journalists are detained or killed in India now than at any other time. And on Index's Index, it scores only seven in academic, media and digital freedom.

These ratings reflect the reality

on the ground, where foreign non-governmental organisations find it impossible to function. Amnesty International had to close its offices in 2020 after the Indian government froze its bank accounts. This followed the group publishing two reports that were highly critical of the Bharatiya Janata Party's human rights record. Donors including the Ford Foundation, the Gates Foundation and the Open Society Foundation find it impossible to fund homegrown charities that fight to defend rights. Even India-based donors are too scared to contribute. They worry about tax raids or questions from the Enforcement Directorate, which can examine every transaction to its minutest detail, and potential donors simply conclude it is not worth their while to support an NGO fighting for Dalit or Muslim rights.

India is a country where 15 human rights defenders who campaigned for better treatment for minorities have been held in custody since 2018 in a case known as "Bhima Koregaon" for alleged crimes which the state hasn't even bothered to itemise. It is the country where, in one state, Muslim female students cannot wear headscarves in class, where Muslim candidates for jobs are unlikely to get shortlisted, and where a Muslim family won't find it easy to buy or rent property. It is where a Muslim suspected of transporting cows is likely to be lynched, and where Hindu extremists making loud speeches calling for a genocide targeting Muslims will not get prosecuted. It is a country where government officials will garland Hindu men released from jail after they've killed Muslims, and the state government will release Hindu men who have raped a Muslim woman and →

➔ murdered her child. These men belong to, or are sympathetic to, Modi's BJP, and the party finds it expedient to keep the cauldron hot.

The targeting of Muslims is systematic. A law intended to identify Indians by citizenship is ostensibly developed to figure out who, among those Indians who aren't Hindus, can prove their legitimacy in the country. If you are Hindu, Parsi, Jain or Buddhist from the countries surrounding India, you get fast-tracked to citizenship. At the same time, those who cannot prove they are Indian and who happen to have Muslim names are sent to camps in India's north-east. While such camps are not similar to the kind of camps where Uyghurs are sent in West Turkestan (or Xinjiang, as China calls that province), these are concentration camps, if not labour camps. Little is known about what happens in them.

Be careful talking about all of this, of course. The BBC was raided for a so-called "tax survey" just weeks after it broadcast a documentary which implicated the prime minister in a massacre. And a journalist has only just walked out of jail after more than two years inside without trial. Siddique Kappan was trying to investigate a high-profile gang-rape when he was arrested, ostensibly on terrorism-related charges. Journalists keep on good terms with the Modi administration or face backlash, in prison, or in many instances online, where the trolls are relentless, especially if the reporter is female.

The remarkable aspect is that the world is riled about what happens in China, for example, but it gives India a free pass. Why aren't more people speaking out? On top of having elections, India's articulate elite speak English, even if with an accent – that might partly explain it. Then there is the fact that ➔

RIGHT: Muslims break the fast during Ramadan in Delhi, April 2022. India's Muslims have been increasingly targeted under Modi

→ India has enormous soft power, thanks to Bollywood, yoga, classical music, curries and its prowess in cricket. The horrors of India are also not as terrible as what happens in Syria or Ukraine. The world's silence is deafening.

* * *

When Nehru addressed his constituents at midnight on 14 August 1947, there was immense curiosity, even joy, around the world. His speech, known as "tryst with destiny", has become widely known for its eloquence and awareness of the task that lay ahead for his nation, which was still suffering a bloody partition. There was understandable curiosity – former British Prime Minister Winston Churchill had even ridiculed the idea of India as a country as "a mere geographic expression... no more a single country than the equator".

When the British left India, it was divided into two wings – Pakistan on each side for the sub-continent's Muslims, and a much larger Hindu-majority nation. India included British India as well as some 500 princely states, large and small, whose rulers believed themselves to be sovereign. There would be inevitable Balkanisation, many anticipated. It would remain poor; Indians would starve; it would be the poster child of poverty – and the choice of its post-independence leadership for socialism only confirmed those fears.

John Kenneth Galbraith, the US ambassador to India during the Kennedy years, called it a "functional anarchy". The economist was right – the key word was "functional". It worked. Against all odds. It had every imagined grouping that would hate another grouping, but it spluttered on.

For a long time, India could carry on – the Cold War showed it to be a country that was, by those standards, "democratic". That then changed. Now many more countries hold elections, however flawed; India is no longer the exception.

I recall a dinner with a US diplomat in Bombay in the late 1980s. By then, Eastern Europe had shaken off the Soviet umbrella. One by one, Soviet satellite states were freeing themselves. Vaclav Havel would soon become Czechoslovakia's (and later the Czech Republic's) president. The diplomat told me, quite frankly: "India's free ride is going to end soon. Until a few years ago, there were a handful of democracies, and most were in the West. You were the exception. Now, with [Lech] Walesa in Poland, Havel in Czechoslovakia, the world is changing – there are going to be many more democracies. They will write liberal constitutions. Their new leaders have been close to the West. And India's flaws – the communal riots, caste riots – will be far more visible."

He was right. In 1990, I went to South Africa for the first time, and interviewed politicians across the spectrum. They admired India. Intellectuals such as Nadine Gordimer, Zach de Beer and Allister Sparks and politicians such as Nelson Mandela, FW De Klerk, and many more I met and interviewed admired India's democracy and Mohandas Gandhi's years in South Africa. Mandela biographer Fatima Meer told me: "You gave us barrister Gandhi, we gave you the Mahatma." The constitution South Africa gave itself was far more liberal than what India had written for itself in the 1950s – although it has passed laws to restrict many of the rights. As British historian

Perry Anderson put it, the "poetry of revolution" has to make way for the prose of administration.

* * *

Since 1925, an organisation called the Rashtriya Swayamsevak Sangh (National Voluntary Union) has sought to write a different narrative in India. Some of its leaders have been unabashed admirers of Italy's Mussolini and of Hitler and Nazi Germany – admiring its "nationalism". No major leader of the RSS ever did anything to make India free. Some of its leaders were arrested by the British, but one of their prominent icons, Vinayak Savarkar, wrote abject apology letters to be freed from jail. Now honoured as an Indian icon, he was charged with Mahatma Gandhi's assassination, but he was acquitted. The actual assassin, Nathuram Godse, was a member of right-wing organisations allied with the RSS. There are politicians in Modi's party who admire Godse – they call him a patriot and films and plays honouring him have been released. One Indian state even considered naming a bridge after him.

The RSS has been banned three times in independent India: in 1948, after Gandhi was murdered; in 1975, during the Emergency; and then again in 1992, after Hindu nationalist zealots destroyed a mosque in Ayodhya because they believed it was built on a site where the Hindu god-king, Rama, was born millennia ago. The RSS has several allied organisations, one of which is the BJP, formed in 1980, to which Modi belongs and which has steadily built its influence – raising its share of the vote to nearly 40% now.

The Modi administration is unabashed in promoting the Hindu faith over others. In a country with 200 million Muslims, Modi has no Muslims in his cabinet and he ritually prostrates himself before Hindu idols and participates in religious ceremonies while unveiling national monuments. India is

 India is now a country where minorities must accept they are minorities and not equal citizens

Architect of oppression

During his nine years as prime minister, Narendra Modi has carefully constructed his public image. That's not the only thing he has built. MARNIE DUKE lists Modi's key architectural projects, which are used to further his leadership cult, eradicate Islam and ensure the ascendancy of a Hindu nationalist agenda

Grand designs
When made prime minister, Modi announced the construction of 10 adivasi (tribal) museums across the country. The promise was used to glorify his public image. BJP party members claimed his commitment to the history of these tribes. Work is still ongoing.

Home discomforts
In 2018 the Kashi Vishwanath Corridor Project was set in motion by the ruling BJP. The project aimed to provide devotees easier access to the Kashi Vishwanath Hindu temple, considered among the most sacred in the country. The project resulted in the demolition of 250 buildings, put livelihoods at risk and caused thousands to lose their shops and homes.

A vain remaking
A project was announced in 2019 to modernise India's parliament and historic centre in New Delhi. The multi-billion dollar reconstruction was branded a vanity project that served the prime minister, not his people. And on the note of vanity, in February 2021 a cricket stadium was renamed The Narendra Modi Stadium.

Gods and mortar
In October 2018, the Statue of Unity was erected, the world's tallest statue at 597 feet, to Vallabhbhai Patel, the Hindu-Gujarati freedom fighter. In November 2021, Modi unveiled a 12-foot high statue of Adi Guru Shankaracharya, a Hindu philosopher and deity. Then in 2022 Modi inaugurated a 216-foot statue of the Hindu philosopher Ramanujacharya, and unveiled a 108-foot statue of the Hindu god Lord Hanuman in the Morbi district of Gujarat. Later this year the inauguration of the Hindu temple Ram Mandir in Ayodhya, Uttar Pradesh, is anticipated.

At war with Congress
Modi inaugurated The National War Memorial in February 2019. He used the opportunity to further his political agenda and attack Congress (a key political rival), stating that armed forces and national security had suffered before his government came to power.

On sacred ground
In August 2020, Modi initiated the construction of a Hindu temple in Ayodhya. The spot previously housed a mosque that was destroyed by Hindu mobs nearly 30 years before, prompting Hindu-Muslim violence that left some 2,000 people – predominantly Muslims – dead.

Villain turned hero
Last year Modi announced the construction of a statue of Subhas Chandra Bose. To many in India, he is a hero that helped to achieve independence. However, he left a mixed legacy as a Nazi collaborator.

now a country where minorities must accept they are minorities and not equal citizens. Many state schools no longer offer meat to children as part of the midday meal scheme, out of a mistaken belief that Hinduism prohibits eating meat, and films with Muslim actors are singled out for boycotts on social media. Hindi, a language spoken by less than half of India's 1.4 billion people, is increasingly imposed on states where it is neither understood nor popular.

The BJP's long-term aim is to make a unitary state following a singular faith and with a single identity, including worshipping a single god. Former Prime Minister Morarji Desai once told me how ridiculous it was, but that's the direction the BJP is headed. Its aim is not the next election, it's the next generation.

As Desai told me one afternoon all those years ago, the BJP wants to convert a multi-everything country into a state with one faith – Hinduism; one god – Rama; and one book – Ramayana. That diminishes India, but that's hardly the BJP's concern. The party wants to remake India so that it is no longer how Nehru described it.

"She was like some ancient palimpsest on which layer upon layer of thought and reverie had been inscribed, and yet no succeeding layer had completely hidden or erased what had been written previously."

It brings to mind the Nazi slogan "*Ein Volk, ein Reich, ein Fuhrer*" ("One people, one realm, one leader") – or in this case "*Ek praja, ek desh, ek neta*".

That might sound a bizarre way to describe the world's "largest democracy" but that is where the country has landed.

Nations can turn mad. The Germany of Mann and Goethe did, in the 1930s. Why wouldn't India? All we can hope is that one day India returns to its origins and regains the spirit that its sole Nobel laureate in literature, Rabindranath Tagore, celebrated.

India is a great adventure, a fantastic experiment. Its current leadership is turning it into a mere shadow of what Gandhi, Nehru and Tagore imagined. That leadership is insecure and gripped by an inferiority complex. Such leaders are dangerous. Their failure to imagine is the ultimate tragedy. Modi is incapable of delivering the change, and a large, vociferous section of the population is in no mood to listen. Like the Greek chorus, we wait and watch. ✖

Salil Tripathi is an award-winning India-born journalist, author and editor. He was chair of PEN International's Writers in Prison Committee and is now on its board

52(01):60/65|DOI:10.1177/03064220231165389

Blessed are the persecuted

As Christians face an increasing number of attacks in India, **HANAN ZAFFAR** speaks to people who have been targeted

"THEY DESCENDED UPON him, raining blows with their sticks, rods and hammers. They killed Ram Niwas."

The inconsolable Pinky still can't understand why she has lost the love of her life, even two years later. Hailing from the Sitamarhi district of the eastern Indian state of Bihar, the 25-year-old (who chooses to use her first name only) and her husband were attacked by a radical Hindu mob which targeted them for conducting prayer meetings in the area.

The frenzied crowd broke into their home while they were praying, severely beating them. Pinky suffered serious head injuries but survived. Her husband did not.

After his death, she was forced by local Hindu extremists to leave her home and now lives in another village several kilometres away.

Pinky blames Vishva Hindu Parishad (VHP), a Hindu extremist organisation close to the ruling right-wing Bharatiya Janata Party, for the murder. "He was killed by the goons from VHP who showed no mercy," she told Index.

Members of the VHP, an organisation tacitly supported by the governing BJP, envision making India a *Hindu Rashtra* – a country for Hindus

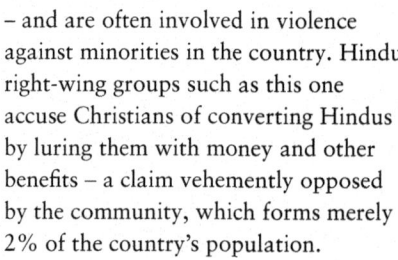

He was killed by the goons from VHP who showed no mercy

– and are often involved in violence against minorities in the country. Hindu right-wing groups such as this one accuse Christians of converting Hindus by luring them with money and other benefits – a claim vehemently opposed by the community, which forms merely 2% of the country's population.

In the northern Indian state of Uttar Pradesh, some 300 kilometres away from Pinky's home in Bihar, the family of 25-year-old Roshan (who also wants to be identified by first name only) faced similar violence. Roshan's father Ram Kishan, a pastor, was attacked at his home by around 30 members of Bajrang Dal, the youth wing of the VHP. Rather than taking action against the perpetrators, the police arrested Kishan and it took his family six months to secure bail from the court. "We are very afraid," Roshan told Index. "We feel like we can be attacked again. There is no security for us."

Religiously motivated attacks like those on Pinky and Ram Kishan are increasing in India. The discernible uptick in violence against marginalised communities has come alongside controversial hardline Hindu nationalist Prime Minister Narendra Modi's rise to power. There have been reports of attacks on prayer meetings and several instances of churches and Christian missionary schools being vandalised across the country.

Thousands of Christians have been forced to flee from their villages as mobs ask them to recant or leave. Earlier this year, in the central Indian state of Chhattisgarh, a mob of several hundred extremists summoned the Christians from one village, beat them and chased them out of their homes.

United Christian Forum, a non-governmental organisation that documents violence against Christians in India, claimed that last year was the deadliest so far for the community in India. According to the organisation's annual report, India saw more than 500 incidents of violent attacks against Christians in 2022, the highest number since the group started documenting them in 2014.

"In almost all incidents reported across India, vigilante mobs comprising religious extremists have been seen to either barge into a prayer gathering or round up individuals that they believe are involved in forcible religious conversions," the UCF said in its report. "With impunity, such mobs criminally threaten and/or

Anti-conversion laws are being misused

physically assault people in prayer before handing them over to the police on allegations of forcible conversions."

Experts blame the government for the persecution. Delhi-based journalist Hanan Akram said: "The government is actively supporting the mobs that attack Christians. It provides them space to operate and never takes any action against them."

Open Doors, a transnational Christian organisation that documents violence on its global community, has ranked India as the 11th most dangerous country for Christians in its 2023 World Watchlist. The report said: "Since the current government came to power in May 2014, pressure on Christians has risen dramatically. This has also seen rise in Hindutva, an ideology that believes only Hindus are true Indians, and that Christians and other religious minorities have 'foreign' roots and must be expelled. Hindu extremists attack others with impunity, using extreme violence in some areas."

An increasing number of states in the country, mostly those ruled by the BJP, have introduced anti-conversion laws to "regulate religious conversions" and critics of the government say they are being used to frame minorities under frivolous charges. "Anti-conversion laws are being misused by right-wing nationalist Hindu groups to target Christians and to use them as a tool of harassment, because it's very easy for

ABOVE: Police stand alert near St Lukes Church in Srinagar, India on Christmas Day 2021

anybody to put an allegation against the pastor or a Christian worker and get them arrested," said Vijayesh Lal, general secretary of the Evangelical Fellowship of India.

And for Pinky, who now lives alone and is consumed by the loss of her husband, the very real impact of persecution has left her at a loss.

"Nobody helped me. Everyone told us that it was our fault," she said. "But what was our fault? To be Christians in this country?" ✖

Hanan Zaffar is a journalist and a researcher at OP Jindal Global University in Sonipat, India

52(01):66/67|DOI:10.1177/03064220231165390

India's Great Firewall

The vision of a 'digital India' has simply been a way for the authoritarian government to cement its control, reports **AISHWARYA JAGANI**

THE INDIAN GOVERNMENT'S emphasis on its vision of "digital India", which was introduced in 2015, has dominated national news for years and has resulted in many changes, ranging from the increased use of digital payment systems to higher internet penetration in rural regions. But this mass digitisation of services has also become a means of allowing surveillance and authoritarianism, and suppressing dissent.

Over the past few years, many government initiatives have leaned towards digital authoritarianism, controlling the data of citizens, gatekeeping access to welfare schemes, excessive policing and censoring of social media, and launching surveillance without a privacy law to protect the rights of citizens.

In February 2021, the Ministry of Electronics and Information Technology introduced new guidelines governing social media and over-the-top (OTT) platforms, which are streaming services. Among other changes, the new rules required WhatsApp and other messaging companies to break end-to-end encryption and identify the first originator of a message if asked to do so. They also have to remove content the government finds objectionable within 36 hours of being notified.

In addition, the guidelines required every social media platform to appoint a chief compliance officer who would need to live in India and could be held personally liable in any proceedings relating to a case of non-compliance with the law. The 36-hour requirement put a lot of pressure on smaller organisations with limited resources.

"This means that intermediaries [are forced] to over-censor, just to avoid liability. And not just financial liability but the potential for one of their employees to face jail time," said Namrata Maheshwari, Asia Pacific policy counsel at Access Now.

Requiring the chief compliance officer to be located in India would enable the government to use pressure tactics, forcing tech companies such as Twitter and Meta to comply with orders to take down or promote certain content. This was evidenced in May 2021 when police visited Twitter's offices in Delhi and Gurgaon after the social media company labelled a tweet by a Bharatiya Janata Party spokesperson as "manipulated media" and refused to remove the tag.

Twitter raised concerns over "the use of intimidation tactics by the police", but has since complied with some of the requirements in the new guidelines. At the same time the company filed a lawsuit against the government in June 2022, challenging multiple block orders on tweets and accounts.

Perhaps more concerning is the section of these rules that requires messaging companies to break encryption. End-to-end encryption enables private communication which is immune to being intercepted or accessed by a third party. In recent years, law enforcement agencies in India, the UK, the USA, Canada, Australia, Japan and New Zealand have been pressurising messaging platforms to weaken encryption standards and allow law enforcement to intercept communication in order to – they argue – prevent crime.

Privacy advocates have been resisting this change, but India seems determined to press on. In November last year, during a visit to India, Meta policy chief Nick Clegg was told that the government would "enforce traceability for law enforcement and security purposes on WhatsApp one way or another". Meta, which owns Facebook, also owns WhatsApp and has legally contested many of the Indian government's recent orders and amendments to rules governing the internet and data.

"This will hamper the ability of Indians to safely access these platforms and have those platforms available to them, which will be a huge loss for Indian citizens if these platforms then decide to move out of India," said Anushka Jain, policy counsel at Indian digital rights non-profit Internet Freedom Foundation.

The emergency powers granted by these IT rules were used recently to block access to a BBC documentary critical of Prime Minister Narendra Modi's handling of the 2002 Gujarat riots. The government ordered Twitter to block more than 50 tweets linking to the documentary, and YouTube was instructed to block uploads of the video – orders both companies complied with.

Other recent attempts to control the online narrative have included the arrests of prominent critics of the BJP, including journalists Siddique Kappan, Gautam Navlakha and Fahad Shah, comedian Munawar Faruqui, activists such as Disha Ravi and, most notably, Mohammed Zubair, co-founder of fact-checking website AltNews.

While arrests and censorship serve →

> The government ordered Twitter to block more than 50 tweets linking to the documentary

CREDIT: Jarosław Zak/Alamy

PICTURED:
A woman in
India checks her
phone, against
a landscape of
data control and
surveillance under
Modi, June 2018

→ to silence critics via the official route, paid and unpaid armies of right-wing trolls are hard at work, harassing critics of the ruling government, issuing rape and death threats and doxxing journalists. New Delhi-based independent reporter Saurabh Sharma, who has received threats for stories critical of the government on more than one occasion, told Index: "This kind of censorship kills the beauty of democracy. Have you seen any investigation that has been critical of the government or exposed them in the last few years in any of the newspapers?"

In 2021, Sharma was targeted for producing a report on Modi's popularity. "Somebody from Twitter had my address, my phone number and details on my family. They started threatening me, saying 'We will come to your house and show you'.

"I found more than 150 tweets against me, containing abusive language and threats," added Sharma, calling his ordeal a case of "digital lynching".

"You can see how [all of this] has impacted us – there is hardly any news organisation doing a fair job today," he said.

This desire for censorship and controlling the narrative has also been seen with internet shutdowns, especially in politically conflicted Jammu and Kashmir, India's northern-most and only Muslim-majority state. For four years in a row, India has held the dubious distinction of being the world leader in imposing internet shutdowns. Of the 182 internet shutdowns around the world in 2021, the Indian government was responsible for 109.

"That's very alarming because India is a democracy. We have constitutionally protected fundamental rights, including the right to be able to express ourselves

freely, the right to share information – a lot of things that access to the internet has a bearing on," said Maheshwari.

Myanmar, the second worst offender after India, imposed internet shutdowns only 15 times in 2021, according to digital civil rights monitor Access Now.

"To be this ahead of a country that's otherwise in crisis should make us introspect as a system, as a government, as people," said Maheshwari.

Many government initiatives over the last few years have leaned towards excessive and often unnecessary data collection, in the complete absence of any law protecting the privacy of citizens.

During the Covid-19 pandemic, the government briefly mandated downloading a contact-tracing app for everyone, which would collect names, phone numbers, health details and location data. The mandate was lifted after widespread public criticism, but the app continued to be required for entry into airports, shopping malls and offices.

Less than a year later, when the Covid-19 vaccination drive began, citizens had to contend with another data-collection exercise, as the only way to access vaccinations was through a website that required uploading one's Aadhar card number (an identification document issued to each citizen by the government), phone number, location and other data. This excluded those without official documentation and those with low digital literacy, and many undocumented people remain unvaccinated against Covid-19 even today.

"There is definitely a trend towards excessive data collection," said Jain.

This disregard for privacy has led to an overuse of surveillance technology, particularly facial recognition tools. While the majority of the world's most surveilled cities are in China, India is

a close second. New Delhi, the capital, tops the list of the most surveilled cities in the world with 1,826 cameras per square mile.

Footage from these cameras is often processed through facial recognition technology, in conjunction with data from official identification documents and other sources, to identify people, with no law in place to protect their right to privacy.

During the nationwide demonstrations in December 2019 protesting against a discriminatory citizenship act, and again during the farmer protests in 2020 and 2021, law enforcement agencies used facial recognition software to arrest and detain those suspected of being involved in protests.

Today, the government is working on building a national face database and a national automated facial recognition system to match footage from CCTV cameras across the country with photographs in existing databases of identity documents such as Aadhar cards and driving licences.

"This kind of use [of facial recognition technology] definitely leads to a dampening of dissent, especially when used by law enforcement agencies," said Jain.

She also raised concern over a "concerted effort to concentrate powers within the government and to remove any reasonable safeguards or restrictions that might be there".

These instances of citizens' data being used in exploitative ways, and the disregard for privacy rights, point to India's urgent requirement for a comprehensive data protection or privacy law. Following a landmark 2017 Supreme Court judgement that identified privacy as a fundamental right, a data protection bill was, in fact, put forward, and is being worked on. But the process has been contentious, with continual efforts by the government to undermine the provisions of the bill and introduce loopholes.

In 2019, two years after the Supreme Court granted citizens the right to

I found more than 150 tweets against me, containing abusive language and threats

privacy, a government-appointed independent committee headed by a former Supreme Court judge presented the first draft of a data protection bill. This draft included fairly strong clauses governing the storage and processing of personal data, and allowed data to be processed only for clearly defined purposes. The committee also recommended setting up an independent Data Protection Authority.

But soon after, the initial draft was withdrawn by the parliament and a new bill put forward. The bill, which continues to draw enormous criticism from privacy advocates, grants sweeping exemptions to government agencies. It is vague and nonspecific, and fails to protect citizens, especially children, against surveillance and non-consensual use of their data. Moreover, the bill, if written into law, will not be independently enforced; instead, a Data Protection Board appointed by the government will oversee its implementation.

"[The current] data bill does not adequately limit surveillance powers in ways that it should," said Maheshwari.

Jain added: "We need a data protection law, but we need it to actually protect the privacy of citizens."

In addition to criticism from local privacy and policy experts, the bill has drawn significant flak globally. Human Rights Watch, for example, stated recently that the bill in its present form will not protect people's privacy and will "enable unchecked state surveillance".

These "oversights" in protecting the autonomy and privacy of citizens are likely intentional. A weak data protection law allows government and law-enforcement agencies to fully use the resources at their disposal to limit free expression and movement, and clamp down on dissent, criticism and protests.

In the last few years, India's reputation as a democracy and liberal society has suffered, as the country has slipped many spots on various indices measuring freedom and human rights. India has been ranked seventh – "partially open"

India's media trials

Journalists have been under constant attack since Prime Minister Narendra Modi came to power. FRANCIS CLARKE outlines the key threats

Arrests
Seven journalists were in prison in India as of February 2023, with many others being investigated or charged under the Unlawful Activities Prevention Act, which allows authorities to categorise individuals as terrorists. Critics say these investigations are politically motivated and used by the government to crush dissent. Another journalist, Siddique Kappan, was released in February after being jailed for two years without trial.

Harassment
Harassment, in particular online, is rife. Washington Post reporter Rana Ayyub has spoken out about the threats she has received from Hindu nationalists as just one example. A prominent critic of Modi, Ayyub reports on issues affecting India's minority Muslims. After accusing Modi of being complicit in deadly sectarian violence in Gujarat in 2002, she also faced legal harassment by the authorities, including the freezing of assets.

Charges
Eight journalists, including the editor of news website The Wire, were charged with sedition after a protester's death at a rally in Delhi in January 2021. They all reported, published or shared the views of the family of Navreet Singh, who believe that he was fatally shot by police. Most of the cases were filed in Modi's Bharatiya Janata Party-ruled states.

Blackouts
Asianet News and Media One TV broadcasts were banned for 48 hours in March 2020 because of their coverage of riots in Delhi. The stations were accused of siding with Muslims, criticising police inaction and accusing Rashtriya Swayamsevak Sangh – Hindu nationalists – of participation.

Searches
In February 2023, after the BBC aired a documentary in the UK that was critical of Modi, India's finance ministry searched the broadcaster's Delhi and Mumbai offices, accusing it of tax evasion. Critics of Modi said it was an attempt to intimidate the media overall because of the documentary.

Sackings
Journalist Shyam Meera Singh was fired by the India Today Group in July 2021 for posting tweets from his personal account that were critical of Modi. The media conglomerate said he had breached its code of conduct policies, while Singh accused Modi of imposing the policies on his former employer.

Takeovers
A final tactic involves making conditions unworkable. In November 2022 experienced journalist Ravish Kumar, known for his hard stance on those in power, resigned from New Delhi Television following a takeover by tycoon and Modi-ally Gautam Adani.

– on the Index Index, a new project that uses innovative machine learning techniques to map the free expression landscape. The country is 150th on the World Press Freedom Index and 119th on the Human Freedom Index.

The new constraints on digital freedom and disregard for privacy and fundamental rights are further tarnishing India's global standing and pushing it towards authoritarianism. Jain pointed out that all of this has led to a "shrinking of civic space".

"The digital spaces where people feel comfortable or safe enough to come and express ideas without the worry of retaliation or harm coming to them have shrunk a lot in India," she said.

Is India still the world's largest democracy? Its digital space would suggest otherwise. ✖

Aishwarya Jagani is a journalist based in India

52(01):68/71|DOI:10.1177/03064220231165392

CREDIT: (top-left) Pacific Press Media Production Corp./ Alamy; (top-right & bottom-left) ZUMA Press, Inc./Alamy

Stomping on India's rights

The members of the RSS are synonymous with Modi. **MARNIE DUKE** highlights who they are and why they're so controversial

RASHTRIYA SWAYAMSEVAK SANGH, or as it's commonly known the RSS, is an all-male paramilitary group and leader of all Hindu-nationalist networks across India.

The BJP – India's current ruling party – is part of the group, and Prime Minister Narendra Modi is a longtime member.

Founded in 1925, the organisation initially sought to unite the Hindu community. But the RSS is now thought of by critics as a fundamentalist organisation that seeks to erase Muslim history and identity in India. The group issued a statement that sets out their mission as "firmly rooted in genuine nationalism" and condemns the "erosion of the nation's integrity in the name of secularism".

Alongside military marches and training camps, the RSS runs thousands of schools across India and its candidates now hold the highest offices in the country.

Modi consults RSS on policy matters. The leaders of its economic wing are

consulted by India's finance minister before the budget is formulated. RSS influences school curriculums, which, in some states, teach Hindu scripture as historical fact. They also influence policymakers to scrap legislation it doesn't like such as the controversial 2015 land acquisition bill that was setback after the RSS expressed concerns about it. Debates about the demonetisation of the Indian currency was also barred from parliament. They encourage the government to "protect" India from big multinational companies entering the country.

Critics argue that the RSS used the democratic process to come to power and now exploit it, by stifling debate in India. The organisation is thought to have more than six million members and influence the majority of India's institutions, including the press and judiciary.

That said, the RSS remains elusive, keeping no records or bank accounts. They also remain distant from their most infamous member Nathuram Godse, the assassin of Mahatma Gandhi who sought to reconcile Hindus and Muslims in India. And at the end of last year they clashed with Modi himself, after RSS general secretary Dattatreya Hosabale criticised rising poverty, unemployment and inequality in the country.

PICTURED: Volunteers of Hindu nationalist organisation RSS march through the streets of Ajmer, Rajastan, February 2023

The photos taken here are all from the same day, 12 February of this year, when the RSS marched through the city of Ajmer, in the state of Rajasthan. The uniforms, the paraphernalia and the crowds are typical of the RSS and provide a glimpse into street life under Modi. ✖

Marnie Duke is an editorial assistant at Index

52(01):72/73|DOI:10.1177/03064220231165393

Bollywood's Code Orange

The Bollywood movie powerhouse has gone from being celebrated to being used as a tool for propaganda, writes **DEBASISH ROY CHOWDHURY**

ONCE UPON A time in India, the release of films with top-billed stars used to be joyous occasions. For days leading up to the release, die-hard fans would organise festive promotions with over-the-top celebrations, often involving ritualistic public worshipping of cardboard cut-outs of their idols. On D-day, they would queue for hours outside cinemas to see the "first day first show" – the elementary test of fanhood – and, once in, wildly cheer their hero whenever he appeared on the screen.

Not much has changed – except the joy part, which has gone. Nobody knows when a new release will be hit by outrage, protests, litigation or worse. This is especially true when it comes to Bollywood films starring its three top male leads – all of them Muslims – who have dominated the industry for three decades. Their film releases have now come to be foreshadowed by ugly online hate-fests.

Foot soldiers of Prime Minister Narendra Modi's Hindu supremacist Bharatiya Janata Party (BJP), who resent the cultural influence of the formidable Khan triumvirate – Shah Rukh Khan, Aamir Khan and Salman Khan (not related) – routinely engineer fake outrages on social media against them. The anonymity of social media gives the ruling party plausible deniability in these well-orchestrated online campaigns, but this January, when an action thriller called Pathaan starring Shah Rukh Khan, the reigning king of Bollywood, was about to the hit the screens, the gloves came off.

The provocation was the pre-release launch of a song-and-dance sequence. In the song, with Khan cavorting with the female lead, he was clad in green and the (Hindu) heroine's skimpy dress was orange. While green is associated with Islam, orange is a Hindu monastic colour (and also the mascot colour appropriated by the BJP and other allied Hindu supremacist organisations), and this was somehow extrapolated into a loaded insult to Hinduism.

Even as engineered outrages go, this seemed pretty silly in the beginning but gradually it began to gain steam. Khan's effigy was burned, and cinemas planning to screen the movie were attacked. Leaders of the BJP and its allied organisations demanded a boycott, or at the least a thorough editing of the film to remove anything that might "hurt Hindu sentiments". In no time, ministers jumped into the fray, with one declaring the movie might be banned because it had clearly been "shot with a dirty mindset". The film certification board said it had asked the makers to make "changes" and to "submit the revised version" before theatrical release.

By the time it was released, Pathaan had become less a film and more a civilisational test of India's multiculturalism. Those astir with fresh sentiments of Hindu pride under Modi declared watching it would amount to pandering to jihadi forces, while liberals urged one another on social media to go and watch it to prove India had not become the cesspool of hate that the Hindu supremacists made it out to be.

This wasn't the kind of buzz Khan needed on his return to the big screen after four years, but much has changed in that time.

Modi's government has become far more brazen in its project to remake India's secular democracy as a majoritarian Hindu state. Brutalisation of Muslims through vigilante violence and discriminatory state action has become commonplace. The mass radicalisation programme spreading hate against Muslims has hit a high gear, and Bollywood has become a key theatre in this campaign for the poisoning of the hearts and minds of the country's Hindu majority against its minorities.

With its universal tropes, cosmopolitan workforce and inclusive cultural representations, Bollywood is at odds with the Hindu supremacists' project. The very deification of Bollywood stars and the visceral devotion of their fans, for example, →

→ cuts across language, religion and caste lines in hyper-diverse India. His fans see Shah Rukh Khan as a star, not a Muslim star.

Indian cine fandom breaks social boundaries just as Indian films often do, with their humanistic storylines. A dispensation that thrives on erecting new boundaries is naturally antagonistic towards such an inclusionary institution, whose cultural influence it both despises and envies, whose soft power it needs to both break and appropriate.

It understands that if India has to be remade, it is essential to remake Bollywood first.

Hindu supremacists appreciate the role of Bollywood in spreading Hindi, their chosen language as India's lingua franca in a nation with 22 official languages and 19,569 mother tongues. But that's no good if Bollywood doesn't speak their language.

Bollywood has in recent years found itself in the cross-hairs of a co-ordinated attack by the regime, the governing institutions it controls, its social media lynch mob and the mainstream media it has captured. Contrived outrages, such as the one Pathaan encountered, have been deployed freely. Amazon was similarly forced to apologise and cut scenes from a television drama directed by a Muslim after BJP leaders alleged it was "deliberately mocking Hindu gods" in a scene in which a Muslim actor dressed as a Hindu god delivered lines they did not approve of.

A cornered industry, forever watching over its shoulder for the next unexpected offence, has responded with utmost caution and self-censorship. A midranking actor (let's call him X – such is the climate of fear that none of the Bollywood insiders Index spoke to wanted to be named) calls it the "sanitisation process" which, he says, operates at every level, from script to editing.

"Legal teams are a key component of all production houses these days, picking up potential red flags," he said. "And every new outrage is a learning point for these teams second-guessing the mob. Basically, the creative space is shrinking with every new production."

Projects have been put on ice, scenes cut, scripts altered, plots picked depending on how "safe" they are, and actors changed. X, a Muslim, says he has never personally faced discrimination in the industry. "But who knows how many projects I have been blocked from because my identity could be a problem?" he asked.

Anurag Kashyap, one of Bollywood's biggest directors, says Netflix pulled the plug on his enormously popular series Sacred Games – featuring a Hindu spiritual leader connected to terrorism and the drug trade – after the Amazon saga, and he believes that he wouldn't have been able to make his earlier films today.

"I have written a lot of scripts but there are no takers. There are no takers for a lot of films which are remotely about politics or religion," he recently said in an interview with The Indian Express.

Airing views like that in public has got Kashyap in trouble, with taxmen knocking on his door several times. The government is as adept at unleashing the troll army as it is at sending taxmen to dig up the money trails of disagreeable films and their makers. Other law enforcement arms of the government are increasingly being used as ruthlessly.

The death of a Hindu actor, Sushant Singh Rajput, in 2020 snowballed, with the backing of Modi's party, into a QAnon-style conspiracy theory movement against a supposedly drug-addled and underworld-funded Bollywood establishment.

Federal drugs and investigative agencies legitimised these concocted rumours of wrongdoing with dramatic raids and arrests of actors on trumped-up drug charges, cheered on by national TV channels. The spectre of drug busts returned the following year when Khan's son, Aryan, was jailed for a month after a dubious drug bust at a rave party, even though nothing was found on him. The message was clear: "Fall in line."

And in order to survive, Bollywood has done just that. The industry's macho men, who once made their careers as action heroes on the silver screen, now openly grovel to BJP strongmen for protection. Groups of Bollywood personalities often meet Modi in highly-publicised "selfie-fests" to discuss nation-building, and industry insiders speak in hushed tones of shadowy figures encouraging Bollywood biggies to make films that better reflect Indian "culture". Their efforts are showing. A whole new genre of movies has emerged that hew to the Hindu right's worldview and promote Islamophobia in the garb of cultural pride.

Films rich in Hindu symbolism or drawing on Hindu mythology are a regime favourite. So are films villainising medieval Muslim rulers and emphasising their battles with righteous Hindu kings. Even though Muslim empires were thoroughly assimilated and indigenised in medieval India, Hindu supremacists view 800 years of Muslim dynasties – such as the Mughals – as colonialism, a period of shame and subjugation no different from the nearly 200 years of British rule. History is being rewritten accordingly in school and college text books, and a whole genre of films has emerged that aggressively pushes this idea that is central to establishing the Muslim as the outside "other".

The children of these outsiders, in the language of Hindu fundamentalists, are

Khan's effigy was burned, and cinemas planning to screen the movie were attacked

not just unworthy of equal citizenship in the land of Hindus, they deserve retribution for the blood of Hindus their ancestors spilled. The apparently innocuous battle scenes in these movies, with beastly Muslim invaders chanting "Allahu Akbar" clashing with pious Hindu soldiers marching to religious war cries and waving orange flags, are designed to provoke a specific emotional response that feeds the BJP's exclusionary politics.

There has also been a profusion of jingoistic films on security themes focusing on terrorism, highlighting the threat from resident Muslims and a hostile Pakistan. The latter works as a dog whistle for Indian Muslims, who Hindu fundamentalists charge with extra-territorial loyalties to Pakistan. Shah Rukh Khan has been called a Pakistani agent by BJP leaders and a "traitor" who "lives in India but his soul is in Pakistan".

These films work to solidify the Modi government's credentials of muscular nationalism – its calling card. In 2019, a Bollywood film called Uri: The Surgical Strike, which re-created a 2016 Indian army counter-attack on terrorist training camps in Pakistan-administered Kashmir, significantly contributed to Modi's re-election campaign. The movie was released a month before the government carried out a new "surgical strike" – an air attack across the border in Pakistan – which whipped up hysteria and unleashed a wave of ultra-nationalism that Modi rode to return to power with a thumping majority.

Like Muslims, liberal intellectuals – a bugbear of the right-wing government – are also often portrayed in these films as internal enemies in cahoots with international forces out to harm India. All of these enemies of the nation are up against the unimpeachable patriotism of government leaders, who bear uncanny resemblance to the current office-holders. The dynamic national security adviser in Uri: The Surgical Strike who suggests attacking Pakistan looks exactly like

ABOVE: A Muslim man rides past a poster of Bollywood movie The Kashmir Files, Mumbai, March 2022. The film has been called a "vulgar propaganda movie"

Modi's own national security adviser.

Sometimes, there's no need for accidental doppelgangers. Some movies are straight-up about the great helmsman himself. An avalanche of hagiographic and reverential Modi-themed films and web series made an appearance before the 2019 national elections. Conveniently, these films contrast the ham-fisted and bumbling past governments. Uri: The Surgical Strike hit the cinemas the same day as a docufilm titled The Accidental Prime Minister – a "shoddy propaganda film" (according to film critic Shubhra Gupta) on Modi's predecessor Manmohan Singh, portraying the latter as a spineless puppet controlled by the Congress party's dynastic Gandhi family (as opposed to the self-made and iron-willed Modi).

A new crop of propaganda films goes beyond merely showing the opposition parties and Modi's predecessors in bad light or "othering" Muslims. The violent

subtext of films such as The Kashmir Files – a film that inflames hatred toward Muslims in the name of telling the supposedly untold story of a Hindu massacre in 1990s Kashmir by Islamist insurgents – puts them on a par with Nazi propaganda films such as Jew Süss and Die Rothschilds.

Hindutva rabble-rousers are using The Kashmir Files, which was promoted by Modi himself and given a tax break, to incite violence. Last November, Israeli director Nadav Lapid kicked up a storm when, as head of the jury of the International Film Festival of India, he trashed the film as a "vulgar propaganda movie".

Later, in an interview with an Israeli news outlet, he said he was shocked by the "combination between propaganda and fascism and vulgarity" in a film pushed by the Indian government.

"It is crazy, what's going on here?" ✖

Debasish Roy Chowdhury is co-author of To Kill A Democracy: India's Passage To Despotism

52(01):74/77|DOI:10.1177/03064220231165394

Bulldozing freedom

Narendra Modi's rule in Jammu and Kashmir has seen buildings dismantled in line with people's broader rights. **BILAL AHMAD PANDOW** reports

ABOVE: People in Jammu and Kashmir hold up documents related to land ownership amid demolitions due to an anti-encroachment drive, 31 January 2023

O N AN UNUSUALLY sunny winter's day in Jammu and Kashmir, a man in his late sixties – Mohammad Subhan Guroo – sat on a bench outside his grocery store. He was lost in thought, until he was approached by a child from a nearby neighbourhood who wanted to buy some sweets. The man hurried inside and fulfilled the request. As the boy left, Guroo's eyes welled up with tears and his voice choked with emotion. He had remembered the awful day when a bulldozer levelled the home where the child and his family had lived in the city of Srinagar, the summer capital of Jammu and Kashmir.

Through the local administration, the Indian government has recently launched an "anti-encroachment campaign" in Jammu and Kashmir. Locals claim to have lost their businesses and homes without any prior notice from the government. Despite possessing documents proving their ownership, they are not allowed to argue their case even as authorities begin bulldozing their properties.

"Before resorting to using a bulldozer to demolish a structure, it is crucial to provide individuals with an opportunity to prove their ownership and present relevant documents," Guroo told Index. "Building a structure is not easy and takes a lifetime for many to complete."

The policy has generated huge controversy as opposition parties claim that the poor and political opponents are being targeted. They claim that 99% of the demolitions are taking place in Muslim-dominated areas. Last year, the administration demolished the homes of Gujjar and Bakarwal – marginalised tribes in Jammu and Kashmir – in Jammu city, the winter capital. The families said the officials arrived without notice to demolish their houses. It was not the first time such a demolition drive had targeted the communities – a similar thing had happened in 2021.

Aakar Patel, Amnesty International India's chair, said: "These demolitions could amount to forced evictions, which constitute a gross violation of human rights."

Jammu and Kashmir Peoples Democratic Party President Mehbooba

Mufti said: "There is *gunda raj* ("rule of goons") in J and K. It is being destroyed like Afghanistan." The police later detained her.

The destruction of buildings on land occupied by people for generations has sparked protests, with arrests being made for stone-throwing in Jammu. A volunteer at a mosque, who wished to remain anonymous, told Index that on one occasion prayer was banned for the day as they feared what would happen should the protests spill over. But with the exception of a few, most people are too fearful to speak out publicly.

More than three years have passed since the Indian government revoked the constitution that provided limited autonomy to Indian-administered Jammu and Kashmir, and New Delhi is directly ruling the region. These evictions are just one of many limits on people's lives and livelihoods that have been imposed in the region. From media freedom to internet access, restrictions affect every aspect of life.

As a majority Muslim region, religious freedom is particularly targeted. India's constitution guarantees freedom of religion, with no discrimination or state meddling, but conditions for Muslims here have deteriorated under Prime Minister Narendra Modi, especially since 2019. The partial shutdown of the region's most revered mosque – Jamia Masjid, the grand mosque of Srinagar – is a case in point. It is now closed on Fridays, the main day of congregational worship, and has faced extended closures for months since August 2019.

Ulfat Majeed, a researcher at the University of Kashmir, told Index he had to be extremely careful when drawing boundaries on maps. After its limited autonomy was rescinded

in 2019, the state was divided into two Union Territories – Jammu and Kashmir, and Ladakh.

"I started my research with the study area of the state of Jammu and Kashmir, and now I have to take care and write twin Union Territories of Jammu and Kashmir, and Ladakh," he said.

Even some of those who once supported scrapping the limited autonomy now feel betrayed. An engineer-turned-educational reformer in Ladakh, Sonam Wangchuk was an admirer of Modi and a strong supporter of creating a new Union Territory in August 2019. Initially, the Bharatiya Janata Party government gave assurances regarding the inclusion of Ladakh under the Sixth Schedule of Article 244 – a legal provision that provides the autonomous district councils with full legislative, judicial and executive authority. But Wangchuk said this had not become reality.

"We were better off [when we were part of] Jammu and Kashmir than today's Union Territory," he said in a video posted on YouTube.

Wangchuk staged a hunger strike in January to raise awareness about the lack of protection for people, land and the wider environment. During his protest the local administration put him under house arrest. It was alleged Wangchuk had signed papers stating that he would not make public appearances, speeches or videos – papers he denied signing.

A legal consultant, Moshin Dar, told Index that the document given to Wangchuk had zero legality and was intentionally vague, so it could not be challenged in court. Regardless, Wangchuk was forced to carry out his protest at home, which diminished its impact.

"The attention of the government

of India should be on protecting the culture, environment, language and tradition of the citizens of India rather than on suppressing the voice of Wangchuk and the other people of the country who are supporting his demand of inclusion of Ladakh under the Sixth Schedule," said Dar. "The government of India should protect the rights of the citizens so that the democratic structure of our country will be cherished."

Meanwhile, the situation has stifled creativity and is diminishing the region's cultural diversity.

Abdur Rehman Rahi, possibly the most famous poet from Kashmir, died aged 97 in Srinagar this year. Revered by many, some criticised him for what they believed was self-censorship. Indeed, he avoided writing on the contemporary political situation. His daughter, Mir Noosheen Nighat, told Index that her father actually *did* write on the contemporary situation of Jammu and Kashmir but just through figurative language to avoid reprisal. He used metaphors to express his views rather than stating them directly.

A filmmaker from Srinagar, Bilal A Jan, who directed The Poet of Silence, a documentary on Rahi's life, agreed. He told Index that Rahi had confided in him about instances where he was threatened because of his work.

Unsurprisingly, the desire for secession remains strong. But to speak outwardly of it is dangerous. Last year, a Kashmir University scholar, Abdul Aala Fazili, was arrested for promoting the secession of the now Union Territory through his writings a decade earlier.

Back outside the shop, Guroo hopes that one day the long night will end. But at the moment, he says, in order to survive it is better to remain silent.

"Speech is silver, silence is golden." ✖

Bilal Ahmad Pandow is a journalist based in Jammu and Kashmir

52(01):78/79|DOI:10.1177/03064220231165395

 ## With the exception of a few, most people are too fearful to speak out publicly

Let's talk about sex

In a country where sexual violence is abundant and sex education is taboo, **MEHK CHAKRABORTY** explores the politics of pleasure in India

WHEN A SENIOR politician in India famously commented that a woman who is raped is a *zinda laash*, or a living corpse, it was in response to the violent gang rape and eventual death of Jyoti Singh, a case that caught the world's attention. Protests broke out across the country as people demanded justice. Sushma Swaraj, at the time the Bharatiya Janata Party leader, made the statement before her party came to power in 2014, and she was eventually appointed the minister of external affairs. She remained an important figure within the BJP until she died in 2019. Her words were illustrative of many public statements by party officials.

"Talking about rape as the worst thing to happen to a woman and not the worst thing done by a man gives the message that, in India, a woman's 'purity' is her sexual trademark and if that is 'lost or violated' there's nothing more to the woman [or her life]," Madhavi Menon, the director of the Centre for Studies in Gender and Sexuality at Ashoka University, told Index as she reflected on the incident.

Around the same time as the Singh case, conversations about sex were also being widely held in India. Paromita Vohra, a filmmaker, writer and educator, told Index: "We saw a lot of content that developed in India was totally taken from the West, imposing a language and context that may not really be culturally relevant."

With this gap in mind, eventually Vohra founded the multimedia sex education project Agents of Ishq, which discusses sex, love and desire through videos, comics, podcasts and other creative mediums. Quizzes and memes sit side-by-side with an erogenous-zones quiz. The website outlines sex education basics, understanding consent and personal stories alongside the Our Erotic India series.

The need to address this gap in the Indian context is especially relevant now, given the rise of the Hindutva ideology that guides the current regime, aiming to establish India as a majoritarian nation with a singular Hindu identity, Menon explained. It hitches to the mythological wagon of Lord Rama, with Hindutva's suspicion over women's sexuality and focus on servitude to their husbands reflecting the way Sita, Rama's wife, is often depicted.

With the emphasis on a specific interpretation of Hindu mythology, the boundaries around sexuality in India – and transgressing them – have varied implications given the diverse identities. The consequences for women who are Muslim, Dalit or queer are also grave.

This is evident in the routine harassment and frequent instances of the sexualisation of Muslim women in India. In 2022, a Muslim journalist discovered that she and dozens of others had been put up for auction online by right-wingers. Similarly, Dalit women are historically disproportionately affected by sexual violence. And for queer women, their expression of desire can mean being forced into dangerous practices such as conversion therapy.

Cultural contexts

Seema Anand, a mythologist, sexual health educator and storyteller, underscores a unifying experience that women in India face: talking about pleasure itself seems to be a major problem, especially if a woman leads the conversation. This, she told Index, is because "if a woman becomes articulate, that unbalances the status of power".

A look at India's diverse cultural, religious and social traditions challenges the narrative that the Hindu right is centring. Menon, who has captured some aspects of this idea of multiplicity in her book Infinite Variety: A History of Desire in India, echoes what many others feel. "We are steeped in a certain colonial mindset of women's sexuality as prudery, and ironically it is encouraged as native to our culture," she said.

The need for a nuanced approach to talking about sexuality is exactly what has informed the work of Agents of Ishq. Vohra said that they operated on a decolonial paradigm, to break the binary approach overall. She invites people to rethink the idea of "smashing" taboos as such. Context has become key to effectively communicating about sex, and for including vast audiences. Vohra joked: "Agents of Ishq is the Shahrukh Khan [a popular Indian actor] of sex education in India," and noted how it uses joyful and celebratory elements of the Indian cultural framework.

Anand, too, delves into the Indian cultural context, highlighting the importance of the Kama Sutra and concepts such as Shringar Rasa, which is the aesthetics of eroticism and romance. She said: "There's an entire vocabulary of pleasure that unfolds with stories associated with each word and act. This helps us understand how, for example, wearing a certain piece of jewellery related to sex. How that jewellery moved on your body taught you how to perform that position."

Anand often shares tales from Indian mythology and makes them accessible to wider audiences. But for those who diverge from the ideal of a chaste woman, expressing desire invites silencing and shaming.

Censoring sex education

Social media has become an important tool for sex educators in India, who

ABOVE: A rare moment of openness - participants in a drive to increase awareness about contraception on World Condom Day 2019, Thane, India

seek to reach vast audiences with limited resources. But it is also where censorship quickly gains ground. Anand said that she has had a very different relationship with her audiences since the Covid lockdowns, when social media became a more important platform. Although a few people within her immediate social circle already shamed her for her work, social media has led to unending attempts at silencing and intimidation.

Vohra, too, has battled with online censorship, but in a different form. "With 90% of our posts, promotions get refused. Because they see sexual content, it is considered as soliciting or pornography," Vohra explained, describing Meta's community standards policies.

Another hurdle is the algorithmic push for polarised views. These policies mean restricted access to information for many, but violence against women remains. Anand found that for many women in her audience, sexualised language is being used as a weapon. She said: "This is not only through direct sexualised threats that the general population hurls at them. They are slut-shamed, called [derogatory terms for] sex-workers, for wanting to even educate themselves."

The road ahead for safe and pleasurable sex lives for women in India remains a long and tricky one. And the idea that it is a woman's role to preserve "honour", for both the state and society, is not limited to India under the BJP, nor is it unique to the country.

"Growth or change doesn't come from simplistic ideas of reform, where some proclaim Indian culture to be great and perfect while some proclaim Indian culture is oppressive and needs to be smashed. Rather the truth is somewhere else – in liberation from these binaries and building on people's complex, lived experiences," Vohra said.

Beyond this, she drew on a powerful belief that Agents of Ishq holds: "If violence is a dictatorship, pleasure is a joyful democracy. The politics of pleasure counters violence." ✖

Mehk Chakraborty is a journalist and researcher from India

52(01):80/81|DOI:10.1177/03064220231165396

Uncle is watching

ANINDITA GHOSE shines a spotlight on the vigilantes in India who try to control women

N APRIL 2022 in Agra – the Indian city best known for housing the grand monument to love, the Taj Mahal – members of a vigilante group known as Dharam Jagaran Samanvay Sangh set two houses on fire.

The houses belonged to Sajid Qureshi, a Muslim gym owner accused of kidnapping a 22-year-old Hindu woman. Indian news website The Wire reported that a missing person's report was lodged by the woman's family, with the subsequent case falling under a law that addresses kidnapping a woman with the intention of compelling or seducing her into sex or marriage.

The Dharam Jagaran group is a member of the Sangh Parivar, an umbrella term for Hindu nationalist organisations led by the Rashtriya Swayamsevak Sangh (RSS). The members of vigilante groups are self-appointed foot soldiers of Hindutva – the predominant form of Hindu nationalism formulated as a political ideology by Vinayak Damodar Savarkar in 1923. India's ruling party, the Bharatiya Janata Party, is also part of the Sangh Parivar.

The mob that burnt Qureshi's house demanded his arrest on the grounds of a phrase that Hindutva groups have lately introduced into the nationalistic lexicon:

The policing of women's bodies and choices starts at home

"love jihad". It implies a conspiracy by Muslim men to convert Hindu women to Islam through marriage. In this case, the couple managed to escape and the woman in question, a BA student, later released a video stating that she had married Qureshi willingly. But that's not the outcome in every case.

In endogamous societies such as India, it is not uncommon for transgressive inter-caste and inter-faith couples to pay with their lives. In a statement in parliament in 2021, the minister for home affairs declared that between 2017 and 2019, the country had recorded 145 cases of "honour killings" across the country. These are usually commissioned by the families of the women.

In my debut novel The Illuminated, an organisation called Mahalaxmi Seva Sangh starts off innocently enough as a "volunteer group to support women's interests". I wanted to illustrate their growth and the articulation of their plans by interspersing the narrative with their posters on everything from what women can wear ("Avoid red clothing") to the more sinister "dangers of women living alone" ("Temptation and sensual

CREDIT: Joerg Boething / Alamy

behaviour"). The posters get more defined as the novel progresses. That is the insidious nature of patriarchal systems. It starts off in small ways, both in my novel and in the reality of India.

Long before groups such as Dharam Jagaran arrive with torches, the policing of women's bodies and choices starts at home. The social legitimacy given to everyday forms of patriarchal vigilantism on issues such as women's clothing and being "allowed" to study, work, travel or live by themselves can escalate to gruesome episodes.

In July 2021, for instance, it was reported that 17-year-old Neha Paswan was beaten to death by her uncles and grandfather in the northern state of Uttar Pradesh for wearing jeans.

Perhaps nowhere more than in India is Sansa Stark's scathing takedown in Game of Thrones, "Uncle, please sit", more vital. In an essay in financial daily Mint, economist Shrayana Bhattacharya has observed that "behind every case of a woman being robbed of her right to speak, live, love, study or dress as she pleases is a type of unhelpful uncle".

Not all commit obvious crimes against women but they endorse the foot soldiers who do the dirty work of upholding the patriarchy.

While it would be fair to correlate the rise of Hindutva with the BJP coming to power in 2014 under prime minister Narendra Modi, these incidents are not entirely new. In January 2009, a group of men from an organisation called Sri Ram Sena attacked young men and women in a pub in Mangalore, dragging out the women and beating them for being "immoral".

They announced a plan to target couples found celebrating Valentine's Day a month later, which led to a widely-publicised campaign by female journalists who organised themselves into the Consortium of Pub-Going, Loose and Forward Women and sent the vigilantes pink panties as part of what they called the Pink Chaddi Campaign. The considerable embarrassment that this entailed led the RSS to distance itself from Sri Ram Sena's activities – a reminder of how political parties and nationalist organisations opportunistically support vigilante groups.

It is crucial to keep the sentiment of vigilantism against women in check at a local community level. Hindutva groups see themselves as gatekeepers of Hindu sovereignty, with a sense of impunity. They operate independently but have a mutually beneficial relationship with political networks.

While the larger focus of Hindutva groups so far has been against Muslims and Dalits as they indulge in religious or caste-based crime – specifically alleged cow slaughter and beef consumption – the focus on controlling women is not far behind.

In a 2021 paper, Sana Jaffrey, director of the Institute for Policy Analysis of Conflict in Jakarta, explains how Indonesian Islamists and Indian Hindu nationalists effectively use vigilante violence to accelerate enforcement of their ideological vision at the grassroots level. Jaffrey believes there has been a shift away from large-scale communal riots in India to targeted activities such as moral policing on Valentine's Day, anti-love jihad squads and more. She warns that right-wing vigilantism tends to be far more brutal and deadly in India as its police structure is susceptible to vigilantes' demands for impunity.

Things get truly alarming when governments start taking cues from vigilante groups.

In December 2022, the state government of Maharashtra instituted a panel to track inter caste and inter faith marriages. To be headed by the state's women and child development minister, the committee has been tasked with

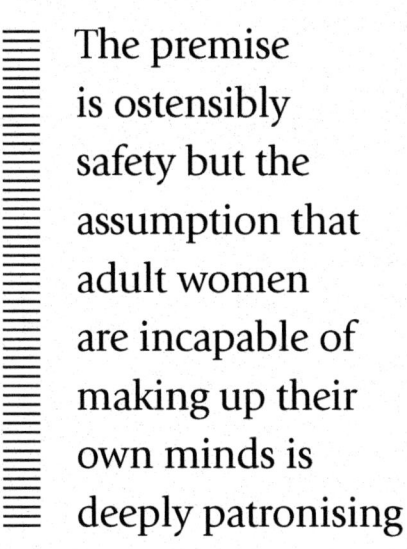

The premise is ostensibly safety but the assumption that adult women are incapable of making up their own minds is deeply patronising

collecting detailed information to "help women" who may be estranged from their families. The premise is ostensibly safety but the assumption that adult women are incapable of making up their own minds is deeply patronising.

The trigger for this move was the murder of a Hindu woman by her Muslim boyfriend in Delhi, but instituting the panel in its aftermath seems more to prove a point: that women are the safest under the care of their families and the state. This is control masked as care.

Speaking about The Handmaid's Tale, Margaret Atwood maintains that everything in the book has happened in some part of the world at some point. That is also true for the actions of the MSS in my novel – there is a vigilante group somewhere in India controlling how women dress and eat and work and live. For readers who see the activities of the MSS as speculative fiction, I wish I had their optimism.

My novel's vigilante group is closer to India's political reality than I'd like it to be. ✖

Anindita Ghose is an Indian journalist and author whose debut novel, The Illuminated, was published in the UK in January

52(01):82/83|DOI:10.1177/03064220231165397

THE ZEKAMERON

ONE HUNDRED TALES FROM BEHIND BARS AND EYELASHES

WINNER ENGLISH PEN AWARD

MAXIM ZNAK

TRANSLATED BY JIM AND ELLA DINGLEY

WRITER IN PRISON IN BELARUS

'It's a terse account of painful experience, prison, bewilderment; hugely atmospheric and extremely funny – full of dry wit and small biting observations.'
- Anna Vaught

MAXIM ZNAK is an international lawyer and member of the Belarusian resistance movement. He was arrested in autumn 2020 and sentenced to ten years in prison in 2021. During his time in Minsk prison he wrote this book which made its way outside the prison walls, and was sent to Jim Dingley, the translator.

COMMENT

"Closing down CIs because of broad claims about the threats they offer will end up making the UK yet more parochial"

KERRY BROWN | KEEP CALM AND LET CONFUCIUS INSTITUTES CARRY ON | P.86

Keep calm and let Confucius Institutes carry on

Banning Confucius Institutes will do nothing to stop Chinese soft power. It'll just cripple our ability to understand the country, argues **KERRY BROWN**

DURING HUSTINGS FOR his ultimately successful bid to be prime minister in late 2022, Rishi Sunak said the UK government would close down Confucius Institutes. This was due to claims that they presented a security risk. Funded partly by an organisation in Beijing called Han Ban, they are linked to the Chinese state. That means that the final command is with the ruling Chinese Communist Party.

There are approximately 500 such institutes – which run China-focused educational and cultural programmes – across the world today. These have been in existence since 2004, and the UK has approximately 30 of them. Last year the Open University opened the first virtual one, but in view of the fact that, overall, the UK has about 150 universities, this is still a small presence to start raising the fears of the authorities.

No one would claim that – in the UK and in other countries which identify as liberal democracies – CIs have been a great success. But the question is where the blame should be apportioned for this. If the aim of the Chinese government originally was to have multiple Trojan horses sneaked into influential entities in the West then it seems to have backfired.

> CIs can work well in one place and be a disaster in another

ABOVE: Graffiti on the sign outside the University of Edinburgh's Confucius Institute for Scotland

As Sunak's 2022 comments prove, CIs have consistently been a lightning rod for criticism and have been used as prime examples by their critics of Chinese official misbehaviour.

Some CIs have been linked to scandals involving staff members intimidating and threatening members of the public and hosting events that promote a CCP-sided view of China. Their staff from China must undergo political vetting and vow to follow Chinese law whilst abroad – in direct conflict with UK employment law. However, an impartial observer would have to be a little more sceptical about many of the grander claims made of CIs.

First, the fact that they are grafted onto British universities and do not have a standalone presence is more of a disadvantage than an advantage. Every UK university in terms of management, power structure and internal cultural is sui generis. No masterplan or template would be able to capture this. If the Chinese ever did have a broad blueprint for influencing the UK through these entities, they must have long ago been disabused of their illusions. CIs can work well in one place and be a problem in another - witness the high-profile closure of the University of Chicago CI in 2014 because of complaints about the terms of the renewal agreement. There are no hard and fast rules. So closing them all down because of the problems in a few places is at best an over-reaction, and at worst unjust.

Then there is the hard truth that once entities such as CIs – with their focus on language and education about Chinese culture – are taken from the picture, there are few other options available for people to get at least some understanding of the world's second largest economy. Many language centres at universities and schools offer some tuition, but it is already well below the amount it should be, unless one wants to make a full commitment and do a degree course. CIs may be problematic but they are also, in part, filling a very under-serviced need. In view of this it is not a straightforward decision to ban them. Nor, in fact, is banning a good look on principle.

Finally, those that most noisily lobby against CIs seem strangely lacking in faith of the ability of people to be able to discriminate and critically evaluate information that comes to them. The idea that CIs are able to brainwash and censor people is a puzzling one. One can

> ## If the Chinese ever did have a broad blueprint for influencing the UK through these entities, they must have long ago been disabused of their illusions

very easily learn Chinese to a high level by reading the speeches of President Xi Jinping. That doesn't mean one would end up believing or being sympathetic to their intellectual content. After all, many people can read Charles Dickens's A Christmas Carol endlessly and enjoy and admire it. That doesn't mean they end up believing in ghosts!

Educationalists, politicians and others are often eager to berate their fellow citizens for their poor knowledge of other countries and languages – and the situation is getting worse. Take-up of A-levels in even European languages is at a historic low. Closing down CIs because of broad claims about the threats they offer will end up making the UK yet more parochial, yet more unengaged with China and yet more insular.

CIs may need improving but walking away from them will achieve nothing, unless the UK commits resources and efforts to replace them with something broadly equivalent. And with the current brutal budgetary and economic situation, we all know that will simply not be happening. ✖

Kerry Brown is director of the Lau China Institute and professor of Chinese studies at King's College, London

52(01):86/87|DOI:10.1177/03064220231165398

CREDIT: Ben Von Klemperer / Alamy

A papal precaution

ROBIN VOSE explores censorship on campus, taking lessons from the Catholic Church's doomed index of banned works

ABOVE: A person protests critical race theory at a "Stand with Trump" event near Trump National Golf Club in Bedminster, New Jersey on 14 August 2022

ONE NEEDN'T LOOK far to find censorship controversies on university campuses these days. All too often, student activists, professors, administrators and outside observers are polarised into rigidly opposed camps. Some claim to defend free speech and academic freedom, seemingly at any cost. Others invoke principles of harm prevention to justify what they see as necessary curbs on certain types of communication. The pressures to pick a side, along with the consequences of making that choice, are all but impossible to avoid for those of us who live and work in the university milieu.

Such choices are further complicated by the political implications of many issues. We are tempted to defend ideas we agree with while condemning the potential dangers of positions we oppose. Free speech, censorship and harm prevention frequently become pawns in larger political struggles.

The notion of harm, in particular, has proven endlessly malleable across the political spectrum. "Harm" is a subjective term that covers a wide range of experiences. Serious spiritual and psychological damage can result from conflict, trauma and abuse, further exacerbated by historical power imbalances. Harm is complicated precisely because it can take so many forms, and for this very reason it deserves to be given thorough consideration. Potential for harm should never be ignored when examining the implications of speech. But neither should it be used as an absolute rationale for justifying censorship.

This is not a new problem. The idea of "preventing harm" was precisely what drove the Catholic Church hierarchy's Index Librorum Prohibitorum (Index of Prohibited Books) to be maintained for more than 400 years. Texts such as John Milton's Paradise Lost and Jules Bois' Le Satanisme Et la Magie were banned explicitly to prevent reader exposure to materials that would (in the censors' judgment) cause them real spiritual, physical and social harm. Milton and Bois were suspected of exposing their readers to potential demonic attack, as were "flawed" exorcism manuals such as Girolamo Menghi's Flagellum Daemonum.

Early modern censors, both secular and clerical, also agreed that "immoral" literature presented a real danger to the health of society as well as to vulnerable individuals. We might now dismiss such concerns as the prudery of another time, but representations of gratuitous sexual violence in the Marquis de Sade's Justine, or the imprisonment and abuse of a young servant girl by her master in Samuel Richardson's Pamela, still have the power to upset readers. Both were placed on Church indexes, alongside works deemed equally harmful for their anti-Catholicism or their promotion of what censors took to be dangerous "fake science". The latter included much truly dubious quackery, as well as figures such as Galileo.

The sincerity of Church efforts to prevent harm may be debated, but their overall failure has become clear even to the papacy. Galileo's case was especially damaging – not only to a talented scientist and the advancement of astronomy but to the Church itself, which was forced to reverse its ban as early as 1757 before publicly acknowledging its error in 1822 and finally issuing a formal apology for such misguided censorship in 1992. The Index Librorum Prohibitorum was increasingly recognised as an embarrassment for this and other reasons long before its final termination in 1966.

The history of the index's combination of good intentions and overreach should serve as a warning. In particular, its devastating legacy is worth keeping in mind as we consider whether (and how) to shield students and others from potential harms resulting from exposure to objectionable writings, ideas or works of art, for censorship inevitably generates its own types of harm.

A case in point is recent events at Minnesota's Hamline University,

Fruitless head-butting over simplistic notions of 'freedom' and 'harm' has gone on long enough

where a Muslim student was offended by an image shown in class. In its zeal to uphold Methodist principles of "doing no harm", the university took drastic action: it terminated a professor's employment and publicly announced that similar discipline would result should class content ever cause offence to members of any religion in the future. This overreaction, unsurprisingly, resulted in a great deal of negative publicity and ended up causing far more harm than it prevented. The student complainant has since been forced to relive the original offence many times. Meanwhile, the entire university has been subjected to threats and insults as well as legitimate criticism. Far beyond one professor, it appears that several other careers will now be impacted, if not ended, by this debacle. The university faces an expensive lawsuit and likely loss of future donor revenue. Its accreditation is being reviewed and the student body and workforce are divided and demoralised. It remains to be seen if Hamline will ever recover.

Similarly, by banning the allegedly divisive teaching of critical race theory in its universities, the state of Florida has unintentionally turned a previously niche academic field into compulsory reading throughout most of the social sciences elsewhere, while marginalising its own educational system in the process. The long-term consequences of such authoritarian impositions on school curriculums are quite predictable, and indeed the current state of US politics already provides plenty of hints at what happens when a society deliberately avoids educating itself critically and openly about important issues.

Harm prevention was never the sole

reason for Florida's ban, Hamline's dismissal or the index's prohibitions. Censorship is also a weapon with which to lash out at some while signalling loyalty to others. All the more reason, then, for academic institutions to avoid taking this route when they genuinely seek to minimise harm while remaining true to their intellectual mission. A focus on "protecting" vulnerable minorities from occasional manifestations of offensive speech does nothing to overturn institutional barriers and practices that actually keep those minorities from thriving on campus. Better efforts and investments could also be made to counter distasteful opinions and nurture alternative voices, rather than relying on coercive suppression alone.

Fruitless head-butting over simplistic notions of "freedom" and "harm" has gone on long enough. What is needed are clear-eyed and historically-informed evaluations of specific conflict situations in all their complexity, wherein the actual wellbeing and safety of individuals and communities can be weighed against the true overall and long-term harms caused by censorship. In the vast majority of cases, such an analysis will show that resources would be better spent on positive long-term systemic reforms rather than on short-term — but ultimately very costly and counter-productive — negative exercises in censorship. ✖

Robin Vose is professor of history at St Thomas University, Canada, and author of The Index of Prohibited Books: Four Centuries of Struggle Over Word and Image for the Greater Glory of God

52(01):88/89|DOI:10.1177/03064220231165399

The democratic federation stands strong

Putin's assault on freedoms continues but so too does the bravery of those fighting him, writes **RUTH ANDERSON**

AS I WRITE this the world has marked one year since Russia's full-scale invasion of Ukraine and nine years since the Russian Federation annexed Crimea. In a world dominated by too much news and too many crises it can be easy for us to move on to the next story, to the next heartbreak, to the next disaster, and allow the abhorrent to become normalised.

But it's vitally important that we do not allow evil to become normal. That we remember how life was before and how it should be. That war and aggression are punished and not accepted. It is only just over a year since we all watched in horror as Vladimir Putin's Russia initiated it's all-out invasion, a year since images of lines of tanks dominated every news report, a year since Volodomyr Zelensky

became a war leader and a household name throughout the world.

The people of Ukraine did nothing to initiate this war. They did not choose violence, but every family is now paying the price for Putin's aggression. Ukrainian families are divided, spread throughout Europe. People are traumatised; they have lost loved ones and too many live under perpetual fear

CREDIT: SOPA Images Limited/Alamy

LEFT: Zelensky speaks at a press conference in February 2023 during the EUCO summit, asking for additional support for Ukraine against Russia

of the next Russian onslaught.

Since February 2022 the towns and cities of Kyiv, Mariupol, Kherson and Kharkiv have become as familiar to us as communities in our own countries. We watched in horror as children sheltered from bombs in basements, as women, children and the elderly were encouraged to leave their homes and flee to different countries. In the last year we've heard stories of humanity at its best as communities came together to embrace refugees, and at its worst as war crimes were shown on our screens every day.

Over eight million Ukrainians have been forced to leave their country and a further eight million people have been forced to leave their homes and move to safer parts of the country. The UN maintains that over 8,000 Ukrainian civilians have been killed in the last year, with thousands more hurt as the Russians bombard urban areas. And as they defend themselves against Russian aggression every person able to fight has joined the military - everyone is on the frontline, whether they are fighting, supporting those who are fighting or just going about their business in towns and cities which the Russians seek to attack.

I make no apologies for standing with the people of Ukraine and with Nato's efforts to support the Ukrainian military. This is a matter of freedom, of the basic right to live in peace, without fear. It is a human rights issue and it is a freedom of expression issue. The war has been as much about values – protecting plurality and rights – as about sovereignty. And so it is a matter for a global charity which takes a stand against totalitarianism.

As president Joe Biden has made clear

throughout the war, Ukraine is now the frontline in the battle of autocrats versus democrats. There are no fences to sit on. Each and every one of us needs to determine whose side we are on and I am a democrat. I believe in state sovereignty, in democratic free and fair elections, in the right to protest, in the right to a free media and the various other pillars that form the foundations of free expression. Putin stands opposed to each and every one of these core tenants of our democracy.

Amid the horror and heartbreak we must not forget the inspirational acts from people who never expected to be on the frontline. The women who came together to feed their communities, the soldiers who freed their families from Russian occupation, the farmers who while under fire ensured that the crops were gathered, the journalists who risked it all reporting the latest offensive. As ever it is their stories which we should tell and it's their pain we should mark.

In the midst of this war, however, it is easy to forget the Russian dissidents, the people who are adamant that Putin doesn't act in their name, the people whose actions will hopefully one day lead to peace. In the heat of war, whilst living under an authoritarian regime, it requires a level of bravery beyond my comprehension to speak out - to challenge your government, to oppose military action, to argue for peace when you live under an autocrat. That's exactly what many Russian people have done since the war began.

We know that the phrase media freedom is somewhat of an anathema to Putin's government and that he has used his "special military operation" in Ukraine as an excuse to close down what was left of formal dissent. As of the beginning of March 2023 Ovd-Info

(our 2022 Freedom of Expression award winners) have documented 19,586 people who have been arrested across Russia for protesting the war. Of those 71% are women. When the cases get to court no one can expect a fair trial; 275 cases have progressed without legal counsel because the state prevented it.

And yet protest continues across the Russian Federation every day. Whilst it's impossible to accurately gauge levels of support for the war, we know that even the most terrifying punishments are not stopping dissent. In late February, for example, Alexei Moskalyov was arrested. His crime was merely to post anti-war messages on a domestic social media platform, to challenge the Russian army over raping women in Bucha and to defend his 12-year-old daughter, Maria, who dared to draw a picture in school promoting Ukraine. That is bravery beyond my comprehension. So it is our job to make sure that those people who are brave enough to challenge Putin and the current status quo have a platform to do so.

Index was founded for this reason, over 50 years ago, when we provided a platform for Soviet dissidents at the height of the Cold War. Our raison d'etre has always been as a space for the persecuted, where the brave and the disillusioned can tell their stories.

The last year has taken my team and I full circle, reminding us of our proud heritage and ensuring that we keep striving to promote and protect the right of freedom of expression in totalitarian regimes.

Today and every day we remember those that have paid the ultimate sacrifice to defend their country, the civilians who have been caught in the crossfire and those brave dissidents who, in the direst of circumstances, keep trying to speak truth to power.

Slava Ukraini. ✖

Ruth Anderson is CEO of Index

52(01):90/91|DOI:10.1177/03064220231165400

This is a matter of freedom, of the basic right to live in peace, without fear

CULTURE

"It's only just now [that] the narratives of slave traders as great men who built our cities is being widely challenged"

MARC NASH | STATUES WITHIN A PLINTH OF THEIR LIFE | P.105

CREDIT: Barbara Bessac

Left behind and with no voice

China's children are told to keep quiet. The culture of silence goes right the way up, writer **LIJIA ZHANG** tells **JEMIMAH STEINFELD**

THE WRITER LIJIA Zhang believes censorship in China starts in the home.

"There's a phrase 'Trouble comes out of one's mouth' – it's common for parents to say this to kids," Zhang tells me. She says children learn early that being a good child equates to being an obedient child and that means not expressing your own views.

We are discussing Zhang's latest short story, which follows a young girl who is raised from aged four by her grandparents as her parents have to work all the time in a factory. She goes from being confident under her parents' watch to a shadow, afraid to speak up at home.

I ask Zhang, given the extreme censorship that occurs in her home country, why she chose a subtle, almost gentle side of free expression to highlight in her story. The answer is personal.

Zhang was born in Nanjing, a former capital city of China, in 1964. It was the height of Mao Zedong's rule. The devastating Great Leap Forward had ended two years earlier and two years later the country would be plunged into the turmoil of the Cultural Revolution, when political stock was all that counted and anyone could easily fall foul of being good political stock. Her father was largely absent, deemed a political enemy and so sent away when she was small (she says she only saw him once or twice a year), while her mother was very much of the discipline-children school. She told Zhang that she couldn't say whatever thought came into her head.

Zhang was also moved by the example of her *aiyi*, Chinese for aunt and typically used to describe personal help.

"It was really sad. Her family was quite poor, so she left her children behind to come to the city part-time. Once I visited her family and I was really quite touched. Her son missed her terribly."

Zhang believes that the combination of attitudes to parenting and circumstance (China's economic upswing has been built by people toiling away from their families) has meant that "parents in China don't know how to be parents".

"They don't know how to communicate with their children. They don't show a softer side."

Zhang spent 10 years working in a factory before turning her hand to journalism and writing. She is most famous for her book Socialism is Great! A Worker's Memoir of the New China, which has been published in seven languages. In her words she describes it as "sort of banned" in China.

"After its publication, I ordered a box of the book from my publisher in the US, but I never received the copies

LEFT: Chinese author Lijia Zhang

- I was told that the book contained information harmful to the People's Republic of China. Therefore they confiscated the copies," she said.

I ask her what she's most concerned about today in China when it comes to free expression.

"So many things!" she replied. "Since Xi Jinping came to power the space for free expression has shrunk, which is really worrying. The media should be given freedom," she said.

"Also I feel gender equality has moved back under Xi. There are now fewer women in positions of power," she said, which is, alas, one of the most visual signs of the backwards trend. Ten years ago two women were in the top 18 in the Politburo; today it is just a row of men. She says that while women have had some gains, such as the One Child Policy translating into more women being educated than before, feminism has never been able to grow into a movement because of constant attacks.

Zhang maintains some optimism though, and hopes that these academic gains will translate into women continuing to fight.

"People do find creative ways to protest," she said.

What of the children left behind in Xi's China? Things may be improving here. Zhang says the pace of migration has slowed – fewer people are moving from the country to the city and that there's encouragement to start an online business if possible, again to slow the pace of movement.

"School is even educating parents to spend more time with kids."

Positive for the children perhaps, but it does sound like a nanny state now within a Big Brother state. Still, if it gets them talking…

Jemimah Steinfeld is editor-in-chief at Index

CREDIT: Jasper James

Children learn early that being a good child equates to being an obedient child

Little Rabbit

By Lijia Zhang

HER PARENTS' SUDDEN departure hit Chunyu like a bolt of lightning from a blue sky.

On that morning, the 5-year-old was playing a game called 'guo jiajia' – acting as family, with her two older sisters in the shadow of willow trees down by the Bala River. In the sunlight, the world looked sparklingly green. Behind them, spikes of rice in the paddy fields were getting heavier, almost ready for harvest. To deter birds from pecking the crops, a row of old DVDs was hung up in strings along the end of the fields. When the wind blew, the DVDs swirled and danced.

Chunyu was given the role of the mother, while her big sister played the father and her middle sister a visitor. Squatting there, she was chopping a bunch of grass with a hand on a stone, pretending to prepare a meal for the visitor. She had become very fond of the game. In Panyu, down on the south coast, where she had grown up, children had indulged themselves in different games, such as "eagle catching chicks", "hide and seek" and "cocks fighting". But this game was more fun. When she'd first arrived here with her parents and her little brother 10 days before, her sisters, who had been living with her mother's parents in this mountain village, hadn't allowed her to take part. She sensed that they didn't like her very much. After all, they had just met for the first time. However, after a week, as the siblings got to know each other better, she had been welcomed to join in the game. And she was thoroughly enjoying herself.

At one point, when she looked up from her chopping stone, she suddenly spotted her grandparents and parents walking down from the village. Her parents were carrying sacks and bags with them. Where were they going? They wouldn't have carried all those bags if they just popped out for a shopping trip. And her mother was wearing her grey factory uniform instead of her embroidered jacket which she had put on at home. Were they returning to their home in Panyu? But without her? She had thought that her parents had taken her and her brother to their grandparents' place for a nice holiday.

As Chunyu sprang up, she shouted: "Ma! Ba! Wait for me." She moved away from the riverbank, and dashed towards them along a ridge, calling out to her parents. They stopped briefly, waving at her. As she neared, the girl saw that her mother's eyes appeared red. Then her parents continued to walk towards the stone bridge, which linked the village with the outside world. Desperate now, she ran at a faster pace. At the end of the ridge, she ran into her grandparents. "Yuyu, good girl," said her grandma gently. "You are going to stay with us. And you'll have your sisters to play with. And your brother, too."

Chunyu didn't want to stay. She wanted to be with her parents, as she had always done. She tried to run after them, but her grandpa grabbed her. She kicked and screamed but grandpa's coarse hands held her like a pair of pincer pliers. Imprisoned on the spot, she watched hopelessly as her parents vanished beyond the bridge. Gone! The girl let out a long wail from deep inside her. She stopped struggling and slumped to the ground. Her sisters came over. Everyone was looking down at her.

She gazed blankly into the field. It looked sickly green.

AFTER THE DEPARTURE of her parents, Chunyu cried for weeks. She felt abandoned, unbearably miserable, angry and above all, confused. What had happened? Had she done something wrong? Why had they deserted her? She wept and whimpered openly at first; she simply couldn't help it. Then her grandma urged her not to cry, which she took as an accusation. And she felt →

Grandpa's coarse hands held her like a pair of pincer pliers

→ everyone, especially her sisters, were laughing at her. So she tried to hide. The only place where she could find some kind of privacy was the toilet in a tiny wooden hut, which consisted of a slit on a wooden board. Beneath it was the family's human waste pit. It squatted beside the wooden house, opposite the pigsty. She spent hours there in the smelly and suffocating toilet, tears falling down her cheeks like rain drops.

Chunyu obsessively thought about the life that she had shared with her parents.

As her name suggested, she had come to the world in Panyu, a district on the outskirts of Guangzhou, one of the richest cities in China. Her parents had been working there ever since leaving their village in Guizhou.

When she was a tiny baby, her mother, a cleaner, had taken her to work, tied to her back. After the girl grew old enough to walk, she was left behind at home, cared for by older kids in the neighbourhood, a common arrangement in the community.

When Chunyu was three, her mother finally produced a baby boy, "a joyful event as big as heaven", as they called it; they had desperately wanted a male offspring to carry on the family line. They affectionately called him Baobao – treasure, a common pet name for little children.

After three months of unpaid maternity leave, her mother resumed working and Chunyu was entrusted with the task of looking after her little brother. It wasn't too difficult. When he cried usually it meant that he was hungry. She would feed him some plain rice, mixed with soy sauce. If he continued to cry, she would feed him rice mixed with sugar. The boy developed an insatiable sweet tooth. Once in a while, with pocket money from her mother, the girl would buy sweets from a tiny grocery store in the neighbourhood for herself and her baby brother.

Her mother sweated away at a factory 10 minutes away. During the lunch break, she would rush back home. Long before reaching the door, she would lift up her grey blouse, her factory uniform, calling her son's name. "Where is my good boy, my 'little treasure'?" While breastfeeding, she would coo about how good-looking the baby was. Then she made a simple lunch, usually, heating up the leftovers from the night before, or instant noodles or steamed rice, with some pickles or half of a salty duck's egg, if they were lucky.

For most of the day, Chunyu would hang out with other children in the neighbourhood, the baby tied on her thin back, the way she had been carried a few years earlier by her mother. In an open area nearby, there were discarded tyres, deserted construction tubes and concrete rings, which provided a wonderful stage for them to play and chase each other. Back then, she was an easy, outgoing and happy child, who laughed readily and chatted unceasingly. Sometimes when she had such a good time with her friends, she would miss mealtime. Her parents would scold her, but never too harshly.

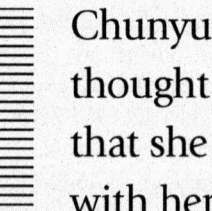

Chunyu obsessively thought about the life that she had shared with her parents

She would stick out her tongue as a way of apology, and then enthusiastically report which games she had played.

Her parents rented a one-room place in a basic one-storey building on the edge of an industrial park. There were several rows of such buildings, standing closely together, as if seeking comfort in this desolate corner of the world. Inside their cramped room, the bed took up most of the space and the walls were patched up by yellowing newspapers. All four of them slept together, her father, mother, brother and finally herself against the wall, always in that order. For the little girl, it was her family home, her secure world.

There was never bedtime reading; her mother, being illiterate, could just about manage to write her own name and her father was only slightly →

→ better. From time to time, as the four of them lay there in the room lit up by a single naked bulb hanging from the ceiling, her father would make shadows on the wall. As he moved his fingers, the shadow of a donkey, a turtle or a dragon would magically appear on the wall. He would tell them stories or songs associated with the animals. The little girl's favourite was a rabbit with two long ears. When the rabbit, with one of the ears chipped – half of his father's right index finger had been eaten by an electric saw at his construction site – hopped about on the wall, he would sing the children the story about a wolf and a rabbit, alternating between a gruff and a timid voice.

WOLF: Little rabbit Baobao, please open the door;
Open the door!
I got goodies and you'll have them all.

RABBIT: I can't open the door. Not at all!
Mama says that when she is not around, no one can go through the door.

It was her favourite song. As she listened, she imagined her father addressing her as his "little treasure" and herself being the little rabbit, bravely turning away the wolf. Chunyu hadn't heard the song for a while. Now being dumped at her grandparents' place, the tune kept ringing in her ears. It brought bittersweet feelings and tears to her eyes.

HER MOTHER CALLED from Panyu and explained that she had brought her and her brother home out of concerns for their safety. Megacities like Guangzhou were dangerous places where "fish and dragons jumbled together", she said. There were a lot of bad people around, who specifically targeted children. They would open their chests and feast on their tender hearts in order to gain immortality. Chunyu nodded as tears once again dripped down her cheeks. She wasn't entirely sure if she ought to believe such a story. But it was probably true that Guangzhou wasn't safe. From time to time, their neighbours had talked about horror stories of someone being

robbed or someone else's son being kidnapped and sold. She never understood why people would buy children. Now thinking about it, they probably did so for their hearts. After a few minutes, her mother started to cry, saying she decided to venture out to work as a migrant so that her children could have a better education and better future. Before hanging up, her mother said: "Listen carefully, Yuyu. You are now a big girl. Don't talk freely as you used to. You must behave yourself."

She shivered. Without her parents, she must be careful now, she told herself. Otherwise, she could be like that little rabbit, easily eaten up by a wolf.

OVERNIGHT, CHUNYU'S PERSONALITY changed. She became quiet, reserved and anxious. She felt like a stranger in her grandparents' house. Acutely aware that she was no longer in her own house, she knew she couldn't conduct herself in the same free and casual fashion as before. Her grandma insisted everyone sat around the table for dinner in the evening. While others chatted, talking about their day, the girl listened, rarely expressing her views. She learnt to make herself less visible; sitting slouched, half-hidden in the shadows.

At night, she often had nightmares where a wolf bared its sharp teeth at her.

Her brother now became the pearl in the palm of her grandma. He had the privilege of sleeping with her; and during the day, he followed her around. Her sisters were also very affectionate with their grandparents. How she envied their closeness, but couldn't bring herself to sit on her grandma's lap or cling to her grandpa's back.

Chunyu stayed alert, silently observing everything; she diligently did what she was told;

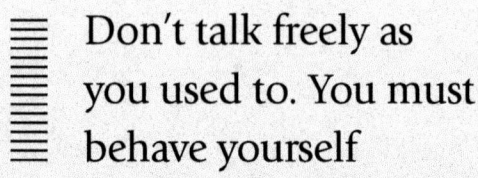

Don't talk freely as you used to. You must behave yourself

Everyone presumed that she had always been like this: pleasant, obedient and quiet

and tried to go out of her way to be helpful. But even her diligence seemed to have displeased her sisters. Once when she volunteered to go out to pick firewood with her grandma, in a throw-away line, her middle sister remarked: "Why do you try so hard?" Chuntao's words gnawed at her. After a long minute, she collected herself and went out, trailing behind grandma.

Although Chunyu liked her grandma who was very kind and gentle with her, it was obvious that she, too, favoured her brother.

She was frightened of her grandpa. He had hurt her when he held her down to prevent her from chasing her parents. He never smiled. He didn't talk much. When he did open his mouth, which struggled to accommodate his large and uneven teeth, his voice was loud and coarse. It startled her.

The only person she felt completely comfortable to be with was her little brother. But he attached himself to their grandma who had the power to give him treats like sweets or roasted broad beans in a proportion larger than those to the girls'. Among the siblings, Chunyu was still his favourite.

It saddened her that her sisters hadn't been warmer to her in the beginning. At night, the three girls shared one single bed, her on one end and they the other. The two of them often whispered something to each other and then giggled. She felt isolated. Why whispering? Perhaps they didn't want to disturb her sleep or perhaps they didn't want her to hear their conversation. Sure, she didn't initiate any conversation with them, only because she was shy and she didn't know what to say to her sisters.

Her sisters, Chunhua, in particular, fired questions at her. What did a city look like? Lots of tall buildings, as tall as the mountain behind our house? Was it so brightly lit that even the night felt like the daytime?

Urban life hadn't left a deep impression on the girl. Chunyu wasn't sure if her neigbourhood was regarded as part of the city or not. She had been to the centre of Panyu several times and seemed to remember some tall buildings, though such things hadn't interested her. She did vividly remember one outing when her father had taken her to a shopping mall where there was a corner for children. There her father treated her to a ride in a plastic car driven by the Black Cat Police Chief, a popular cartoon character. When the car moved, the siren sounded and she squealed with delight. That was her most exciting city experience.

"Wow! You are so lucky!" her middle sister exclaimed, glaring at her. "You've been to a shopping mall; taken a train ride; and you had our parents looking after you in the city while we were left behind in the village."

Chunyu bit her lip. She didn't feel lucky at all, but she could understand her sister's bitterness. She had heard that her parents left home in a hurry when Chuntao was only six weeks old.

Her sisters also asked her what kinds of foods she had enjoyed down in the south, perhaps with mountains of meat and sweets? Chunyu admitted that she had eaten lots of sweets, just that they had been the cheapest types of hard candies, not the exotic-flavoured types in fancy wrappings that her parents had brought home. And when she told her siblings that the food at home was better and tastier, her sisters exchanged a surprised glance at each other.

Chunyu slowly settled in her grandparents' house. No one really knew what she had been like before and everyone presumed that she had always been like this: pleasant, obedient and quiet.

CHUNYU STEPPED THROUGH the gates of her preschool, tightly holding onto her grandma's hand. Then she saw a boy, bigger and taller than she was, wailing and holding onto his grandpa's legs as he refused to go into the school. It made the girl feel better: she wasn't the only one who was feeling anxious about school.   →

→ The children ought not to have worried. The tiny preschool, with fewer than two dozen students, was relaxed. It was a brick bungalow, around the corner from the stone bridge. The children were divided into three groups, according to their age, and taught by two teachers, so that at any given time students from one class had to self-study. When they had a teacher's attention, they learnt to write a few characters, do a little arithmetic and sing a few songs.

Chunyu began to like her school. In her classroom, everyone was equal, and among her fellow students, she didn't feel like an outsider the way she felt at home. She was still shy and quiet, but she made friends with her classmates. They chatted, shared their secrets and laughed. Now and then, she expressed her views.

Her transition to primary school went

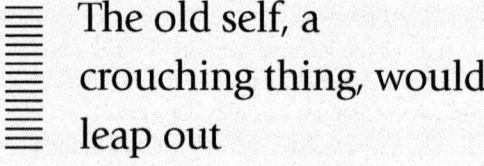

The old self, a crouching thing, would leap out

smoothly too. There she discovered that she had a natural knack for numbers. At first, she hesitated to raise her hand to answer her math teacher's questions, but she gradually grew more confident in doing so. After a while, her math teacher would automatically turn to her, expecting her to offer an answer, which was usually correct.

She looked forward to going to school. As soon as she entered its gate, the old self, a crouching thing, would leap out. She was cheerful again, chatty and outgoing. Her academic success gave her more confidence and she won the respect of her teachers and students alike.

On a bright autumn day when she was in grade two, the math teacher asked a very difficult question to the students. There are 20 persimmons. Little Flower gave away eight to her friends and she wanted to divide the rest equally

among her parents and herself. How many did she have? As soon as Chunyu worked out the answer, she threw her arm up. At home, she had often helped her eldest sister to divide the food, such as roasted broad beans or waxberries, equally among the siblings, even though the brother would always somehow end up eating more than his fair share.

The teacher, a skeleton of a man with round black glasses, surveyed the classroom. "Anyone else?"

All the rest of the hands firmly rooted on their desktops. The teacher pointed a finger at Chunyu with his pointer. She jumped up. "Four!" she replied, nerves fluttering like a butterfly.

The teacher waved his pointer, in an exaggerated suggestion of approval. "Do you mind coming over here and demonstrating on the blackboard how you worked it out?"

Now all eyes fixed on Chunyu. Her cheeks burned red. She hesitated for a moment before going to the front of the class. She was unaccustomed to being under the spotlight. When she picked up the chalk, her hand trembled. She told herself to calm down and focus on the task at hand. Then she wrote out two lines on the blackboard:

"$20-8=12$"

"12 divided by 3 equals 4"

She turned to her teacher. He applauded. The classmates joined in the clapping. Her face was glowing like a red lantern and so she lowered her head. But then she raised it to look at her class, smiling timidly and proudly, her back straight.

Soon, the bell rang to signal the end of the lesson. Chunyu came out to the playground. Sunlight flooded the outside. The world sparkled with promise.

The next class happened to be physical education. Since it was a nice day, their teacher awarded them with free play. Chunyu and her classmates ran wild in the grounds, chasing each other. In high spirits, she burst into singing:

Little rabbit Baobao, please open the door;
Open the door!
I got goodies and you'll have them all.

When she realised she was singing her old

favorite, she stopped, laughing at herself.

With a flash of inspiration, she said to a few girls around her: "Why don't we play 'cock fighting'?"

Chunyu had never taken any initiative to suggest a group game, least of all one that was usually played by boys. "Cock fighting" meant that one would lift up a leg, rest it on the other and use the protruding leg as a weapon to hit others. It was usually the reserve of the boys.

The leader of their group shot a look at Chunyu and said: "Why not?"

The rest of the girls then responded enthusiastically. Being small, the girl was in a disadvantaged position. But she fought with spirit, giggling all the time, even when she was bumped to the ground. She picked herself up and carried on. She felt that that old self – carefree, confident and cheerful – had resurfaced.

Chunyu skipped and sang as she headed home, rehearsing how to report to her family about the day's triumph. She toyed with the idea of informing her parents, but quickly dismissed it. They didn't really follow her daily life or academic achievements. To save money, they reduced the phone call from once every month to once every two or three months. Her mother usually did the talking. She would spend half of the time reminding them of the hardship she was enduring and the rest of the time just urging her children to study harder and take up more housework. Her parents had become background in her life.

To dispel this unpleasant thought, she looked around her. It was a beautiful day. Autumn had dyed the world gold. The wheat fields billowed in the breeze, as if waving at her and cheering her on. With an extra spring in her step, Chunyu ran all the way home. As soon as she crossed the threshold of the house though something about the familiar setting made her revert to that timid self. Individually, she liked each member of her family. By then, she had learnt to get along with her sisters. She looked up to her eldest sister and respected her authority and eagerly took up any assigned task. She had also bonded with Chuntao, only one year older, and she admired the middle sister's confidence and feistiness. Yet Chunyu was never relaxed enough to be herself at home.

The girl found her grandma in the kitchen, busy making pig feed. In a flat tone devoid of excitement or joy, Chunyu briefly described her victory today. Her grandma, usually engaged and responsive, failed to pick up the significance of the story. She just mumbled "well done" and carried on with her work.

In the evening, Chunyu sat quietly at the dinner table, her back, once again, hunched. The halo of her glory had faded away.

Retiring to their bed, she thought about relating the story to her sisters as she wanted them to share her joy and achievement. Would her victory upset the eldest sister, who wasn't doing so well academically? She also feared that Chuntao might accuse her of showing off. The older sisters were still closer allies.

In the end, Chunyu remained silent. Her thoughts turned to that cramped room she had

The halo of her glory had faded away

shared with her parents and little brother. Gone now, those days. She turned over in bed. At least there was school. Wrapped in a comfort blanket, she drifted off to sleep. In her dream, she heard the little rabbit song once again.

WOLF: Little rabbit Baobao, please open the door;
Open the door!
I got goodies and you'll have them all.

RABBIT: I can't open the door. Not at all!
Mama says that when she is not around, no one can go through the door. ✖

Lijia Zhang is a Chinese writer. She is the author of Socialism Is Great!: A Worker's Memoir of the New China and Lotus

52(01):94/101|DOI:10.1177/03064220231165401

Zimbabwe's nervous condition

TSITSI DANGAREMBGA tells **KATIE DANCEY-DOWNS** about Zimbabwe's upcoming election, being arrested for a simple protest, and her most liberating writing experience yet

T IS THE year 2114. For the very first time, somebody in Norway's Deichman Bjørvika library opens the glass drawer etched with "Tsitsi Dangarembga" and lifts out the manuscript Narini and her Donkey, never before read. More drawers contain unseen books. One is labelled "Elif Shafak", another "Margaret Atwood" and another "Han Kang".

PICTURED: Tsitsi Dangarembga (centre) is applauded as the 2021 winner of the Peace Prize of the German Book Trade on 24 October 2021 in Hessen, Frankfurt

CREDIT: (main) Thomas Lohnes/epd-Pool/dpa picture alliance/Alamy; (portrait) Hannah Mentz

A new writer's drawer has been added every year. In this imagined future, a century since the start of the Future Library project, the stories are printed on paper harvested from 1,000 specially grown trees in the Nordmarka forest, facing the library. Art, sustainability and free expression meet.

"I wish you could see the big smile on my face, because it is one of the

most liberating pieces of writing that I have done," said Dangarembga, the Zimbabwean filmmaker and author who was shortlisted for the 2020 Booker Prize and was a founding member of PEN Zimbabwe. "There's no one to tell me, 'No, you represent a certain group', or someone to tell me that it's uninteresting, the names are unpronounceable... things that I come up against again and again."

Short of leaps in medical science, most readers of this issue of Index will never read any of these works. The story is a complete secret. Dangarembga does divulge that "*narini*" means "forever" in what is known as Shona – a language of colonial convenience harking back to the 19th century, when people were "just lumped together for the convenience of the British colonial enterprise". In reality, there are many different dialects.

It might be difficult to imagine what the world will look like in a century's time. Dangarembga herself has a theory, having come freshly out of a seminar about global warming before speaking to Index. She heard about strategies being researched to solve the problem, including one idea funded by Bill Gates in which particles are released into the stratosphere to reduce global warming, known as solar geo-engineering.

"But one of the problems with that is that what you send up comes down," she said. "And so one of the questions that I asked is, 'Is every part of the world equally capable of dealing with those particles when they descend?' And of course, the answer is 'No'."

For the sake of argument, she imagines that global warming has indeed been reduced by solar geo-engineering.

"By the time that these books are read in 2114, I imagine that the most vulnerable people in the world would have been made more vulnerable. I imagine that those areas of vulnerability will have been taken over completely

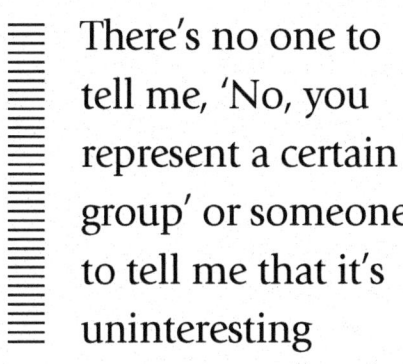

> There's no one to tell me, 'No, you represent a certain group' or someone to tell me that it's uninteresting

by the system of white supremacist capitalism that we live in," she said, whilst hoping that increased migration will at least lead to more tolerance.

In her imagined future, when people open Narini and her Donkey they will ask "Was it really like that?" Just, she said, as young Zimbabweans today ask their parents the same question when they discover her 1988 debut novel Nervous Conditions, which has threads of her early life running through the book's protagonist, Tambu.

In writing Nervous Conditions, Dangarembga became the first Black woman from Zimbabwe to publish a novel in English. As a child, she discovered that words had power. Unsure of why she had been sent to live with a foster family whilst in England, she witnessed the action that resulted from talk amongst adults.

"I realised I was powerless, which meant I needed power, which in turn meant I needed words," she writes in her latest book, Black and Female – an essay collection which deals with the intersection of race and gender that have informed, but not constrained, her writing.

She writes: "There are wounds that burst open as I write. I write to raise mountains, hills, escarpments and rocky outcrops over the gouges in my history, my societies and their attendant spirits."

In 2020, Dangarembga was arrested for six words on a placard: "We want better. Reform our institutions."

"I had disobeyed a presidential ➜

→ decree," she said, describing her protest that so infuriated Zimbabwe's authorities.

In the midst of an economic crisis that Zimbabweans have been feeling for decades, Dangarembga describes life as being "practically unliveable", despite her relative privilege. "If I am in such a position, what about the ordinary person in Zimbabwe?" she said.

In the days before a planned demonstration calling for political reform, interest in it grew, she explained. This worried the authorities. A political decree, under the guise of Covid-19 restrictions, banned the demonstration.

"We had been forbidden to go out onto the street and we had been told to stay at home," she said. "Apparently, they said that if anybody is out demonstrating, whatever happens to them will be their own fault."

Despite the decree, Dangarembga stood by the wording of the constitution that states Zimbabweans have the right to demonstrate peacefully. She even had the relevant paragraph saved on her phone while she protested. If the police challenged her, she'd show it to them.

"I had to have a conversation with myself about what I was going to do," she said. "I felt that, as I had been vocal publicly, to then allow myself to be intimidated by an unlawful decree really would take us back to systems like medieval Europe."

Dangarembga never intended to do anything illegal. She wanted to meet other Zimbabweans and publicly express an opinion. Meanwhile, the treatment of critical voices in the country was firmly in her mind. Ahead of protests in 2019, unknown men with AK-47s abducted and attacked activists while the internet was simultaneously shutdown.

Just a week before the 2020 protest where Dangarembga was arrested, security forces broke into the home of Hopewell Chin'ono, a journalist accused of planning the protests, and arrested him without producing a warrant. Dangarembga had called for his release. (By January 2021, he had been arrested

for the third time in six months.)

"We had this idea that we would demonstrate in small groups so that we could not be called a crowd or a meeting," she said. "What I did not know at the time, which I found out afterwards, was that in Zimbabwean law, a meeting is more than one person."

She and journalist Julie Barnes took their peaceful protest down the Harare streets.

"For me, it was to show my reliance on the constitution and to show how important it is for citizens to have agency and be able to express their opinions in public," she said.

But flying in the face of the decree meant they were descended on "with a sledgehammer". Dangarembga and Barnes were arrested and herded onto an imposing grey police truck.

When the trial started, Dangarembga was glad to be outside Zimbabwe, after being offered a fellowship at the Harvard Radcliffe Institute. A writer's job is to sit and think all day, she said, and that would have been very uncomfortable.

In September 2022, both women were convicted of inciting violence and given custodial sentences. Dangarembga paid a fine to avoid one part of the sentence, and will face a six-month sentence if she reoffends within the next five years.

The ruling Zanu PF party has been in power since the country's independence in 1980, when colonial rule ended but left a deep mark. In summer 2023, Zimbabwe will head to the polls. Ahead of this, president Emmerson Mnangagwa is planning to sign the Private Voluntary Organisation Bill into law, which would mean NGOs could have their registrations cancelled if they are deemed to have political affiliation.

Dangarembga – who also runs a trust, the Institute of Creative Arts for Progress in Africa – believes there is a political strategy at play, with several tactics operating simultaneously.

One of them is propaganda. Due to expensive data, she explained, many people cannot access social media and

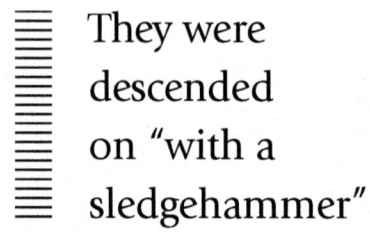

They were descended on "with a sledgehammer"

instead rely on traditional media – outlets which have to buy licences from the government.

"People are not really able to get much information about a different point of view from the government's point of view," she said. "If the government tells them that these private voluntary organisations are puppets of the West, and they're here to destroy the liberation that we fought so hard for, people will tend to believe it."

But even more concerning for Dangarembga is the power that this law would give the government. She compares it to land reform, where the government seized private property.

"It is a very logical consequence of the position that Zanu PF has taken of total control, and they say it very openly – they say 'Zanu PF will rule forever'."

With the election looming, Dangarembga believes that people can make choices according only to what they know. If they are told that failure to comply will result in a lack of seeds for the planting season, they can make a decision based only on the welfare of their families.

"When one looks at the reality on the ground in Zimbabwe, it's easy to think 'Well, why don't the citizens vote them out?'" she told Index. "But one has to know what they're dealing with."

Dangarembga's words, whether fiction, nonfiction or scribed on a placard, go a long way to scratching at the wounds inflicted on Zimbabweans. ✖

Katie Dancey-Downs is assistant editor at Index on Censorship

52(01):102/104|DOI:10.1177/03064220231165402

Statues within a plinth of their life

Can you imagine a world without statues? And what might fill all those empty plinths? **MARC NASH** talks to **FRANCIS CLARKE** about his new short story, which creates exactly that

NDEX IS OVER half a century old, with a massive archive, but for all our amazing writers, famous names and challenging pieces, you'd be hard pressed to find the likes of Eric Morecambe and Norman Wisdom rubbing shoulders on these pages with Lenin, Stalin and Marx (Karl, that is, though by this point you would be forgiven for thinking Groucho). Thanks to the author Marc Nash, through his short story Iconocatalysm, you now can. His story is a satirical look at statues, in which people become frenzied in their desire to topple them. Through the story Nash questions whether we should even have statues. So, why do we?

"Statues can represent different things to different people. Eric Morecambe was a hometown hero. I think it's legitimate to memorialise that after his death. Whereas Stalin, Lenin, Saddam Hussein, fill in any dictator you want, it's in their lifetime and not done as a memorial, it's done as a statement of power. To me, it is

ABOVE: Author Marc Nash

a completely illegitimate use of statues."

Nash is a London-based novelist focused on literary fiction. Described as devoted to the experimental, his novel Three Dreams in the Key of G was nominated for the Guardian's 2018 Not The Booker Prize.

The title of his new short story, written exclusively for Index, is a portmanteau of iconoclasm and cataclysm. It refers to the spate of statue removals (by different methods) sparked by the worldwide protests following the death of George Floyd, and the subsequent division it caused. Broadly speaking, to one side history was being airbrushed, on the other it was being revised. Or, as some argued, history was even being made.

Nash wrote the story following a left-field idea.

"I thought the way round this issue is just not to have any figurative art on display, that the plinths and pedestals should just have some abstract sculptures on them," he said.

"I think it's worth recognising people who made contributions to humanity. However, the nature of power, however well-meaning and intended, means politicians and leaders

are making decisions that affect people's lives for the worse. Why should they get a memorial?"

Nash calls the statues of slave traders "manufactured history", but questions whether their removal will have any impact on the narrative of history.

"It's the wealthy person's version of history, and it's only just now [that] the narratives of slave traders as great men who built our cities is being widely challenged."

"I suspect it will be business as usual, as these movements will be crushed somehow, so the history of pulling down statues will have a hooligan narrative. However, history is made by the winners, so if these protests successfully continue, they can proudly talk about hauling down statues," he continued.

Finally, Nash says statues are more about the message than the art, so would he criticise the sculptor of a statue he disagrees with?

He said: "I can criticise, but I can't say they have no right to. If I was asked to create a statue of Mrs. Thatcher, I would refuse in the blink of an eye, but the next sculptor might need the money!"

Francis Clarke is editorial assistant at Index →

Iconocataclysm

By Marc Nash

AS WITH SO many ideas and gestures in Great Britain, the impetus first emerged abroad. Images of jubilant Iraqi citizens hauling down statues of Saddam Hussein left their mark on the British imagination. And while few recalled iconographic evidence of de-Stalinisation, they did retain memories of post-Soviet Potter's fields of action poses and busts of Lenin and Marx, turning to rust like the Black Sea fleet. We rather prided ourselves for our eight hundred years of Parliamentary democracy, so much so that we were devoid of representations of tyrants and despots. However we did honour in stone and bronze slave traders, colonisers, swashbuckling privateers going abroad in the name of the monarch and other globetrotting belligerents.

Iconoclasm became the new optimal selfie opportunity. Photobombing the toppling of an erstwhile big cheese, lariat around the neck being tugged by hipsters with cordage braced around their hips. One hundred and seventy-five po-faced likenesses of Queen Victoria were abdicated from their podiums up and down the country, where all were amused. A pressgang in Plymouth made Sir Francis Drake's bronze walk the plank and plummet to the Hoe, with the cheering being heard all the way back in Cadiz. But very quickly dissenters jumped to the defence of the effigies, protesting that such acts were erasing British history.

"If only that were true, if only we could reset our shameful, inglorious past," proclaimed the reverse-lynchers. "But what we can no longer permit is to rub the victims' noses in it every day they walk past and have to see this suppurating eyesore." "I think you'll find that what you call 'suppurating' is in fact bird droppings and verdigris." "Even more of a marker of their antiquated and obsolescent nature and the need for a cleansing then," came the retort.

A dissenter bound himself to a targeted statue in an attempt to stay its execution. The symbol of a white man in chains tethered to a slave trader incensed the crowd and they redoubled their efforts, hoping to bring the heavy marble down on the semiotically obscene squatter. But like greenhorn lumberjacks, they were ignorant of Newtonian mechanics and only succeeded in conferring life-changing injuries upon two of their own.

Why confine orgies of destruction to those of so-called high moral tone? Those whose moral compass failed to acknowledge by degrees the relativity of there being three different northerly points. Anyone can become self-appointed. Rivalrous small towns made sport of removing their neighbours' venally venerated mayors and other dignitaries' likenesses, whom not even the host population could have named. Football fans snuck off to their local rivals to cull their sporting gods minerally memorialised. There were only two exceptions to this; one for the captain of the World Cup winning team, local divisions soothed and displaced by international triumph, as touted by Lord Palmerston and George Orwell, both of whose statues also succumbed to the rampant decline and fall; the second for a rendering in sandstone by a journeyman mason, of a millionaire mercenary of renowned prowess who'd laid his Beanie hat there for a few seasons, which was so aesthetically displeasing that it not only bore no resemblance to the subject, but barely matched the notion of a human form at all. Thus it was spared.

A public debate similarly opened up over The

 Images of jubilant Iraqi citizens hauling down statues of Saddam Hussein left their mark on the British imagination

Came the time when all the plinths, podiums and platforms were devoid of statuary

Angel of The North. Ultimately it was agreed that since the angel was not any injudicious commemoration of a real person it ought to be preserved for its aesthetic appeal. The community of sculptors and metal casters were irate since they viewed every last one of their commissions as artistic. Yet they bit their tongues, for they knew they would soon be cashing in on whatever replacements were deemed suitable for the now empty plinths.

Nevertheless, elevated art and exalted artists still suffered from the razing frenzy. In Stratford-upon-Avon, Shakespeare's statue was bowdlerised from its pedestal. The three fictional characters from Robert Louis Stevenson's Kidnapped were themselves snatched from their perch in Edinburgh, without any ransom being demanded. Norman Wisdom's memorial on the Isle of Man took a final pratfall (and was quietly shipped off to Albania in response to a request from authorities there), while Eric Morecambe's statue in, well, Morecambe, was given no more sunshine as it was eclipsed and tossed into the sea to harvest cockles.

Nor were great thinkers and innovators immune. Newton's effigy was rusticated from the chapel at Trinity College by the Kulturkriege mob, while his memorial in Grantham was pelted not by apples, but by sledgehammers. They were egged on by a group of German tourists, who, it later emerged, were members of Gottfried Leibniz's appreciation society seeking restitution after three-hundred and eleven years. A somewhat hollow victory, since they were unaware that their own man's image in Oxford had also come a cropper as part of the cognoscenti cull. Jeremy Bentham's auto-icon briefly gave University College students pause for thought, as they deliberated whether it actually constituted a statue, or was more of a mummy. In the end they decided upon a utilitarianism of being safer rather than sorry and set fire to it, the wax head going up like a Catherine wheel. A certain queasiness did abound over the optics of black holing Stephen Hawking's bust, even though the depiction didn't include his wheelchair, but he too was launched over the event horizon.

Now, a statue is a statue, which is why even though this surge of Jacobins largely inclined towards the Left of politics, they proceeded to attack Karl Marx's bronze and marble, giving him a rare distinction of being vandalised by both sides of the political spectrum. It thus disproved his switching up of Hegel's dialectical idealism to his own brand of dialectical materialism, since an attack on the mineral embodiment of him as somehow representative of his philosophy failed to expunge it from history. The same could not be said for his tomb, now lying in shards; the primitive but persistent technology of hammers and chisels having succeeded, where two attempted bombings had failed in the 1970s.

Came the time when all the plinths, podiums and platforms were devoid of statuary. Even Nelson's Column only offered up his missing eye and amputated arm, reducing it to an uninhabited giant stylus. A spokeswoman emerged from the ranks of sculptors and metal casters champing at the bit with their chisels and forges. She suggested that to avoid any such revisionist repetition wave in the future only non-figurative forms should adorn the vacant mountings. No one could object to that. Cones could happily coexist with cubes and cylinders. And thus was the legacy of Euclid honoured and esteemed, even without a single direct sculpture of his likeness in existence. ✖

Marc Nash is a London-based writer. His novel Death Of The Author (In Triplicate) will be published by Corona/Samizdat in spring 2023

52(01):105/107|DOI:10.1177/03064220231165403

LEFT & RIGHT: The London performance of Crimea, 5am, a play which seeks to highlight the plight of Crimea's Tatars

Crimea's feared dawn chorus

A new play, excerpted below, takes audiences inside the home and families of Crimean Tatars as they are rounded up. **MARTIN BRIGHT** speaks to those behind it

THE TITLE OF the play Crimea, 5am refers to the time in the morning the authorities choose to raid the homes of activists in the Russian-occupied territory. It is a time of fear and horror for the Crimean Tatars, whose voices make up the text of this verbatim work, taken from the testimonies of the men now held in Vladimir Putin's prisons and the families waiting at home for them.

Crimea, 5am brings to life one of the lesser-known aspects of the brutal war in Ukraine, which began not in February 2022 but in February 2014. It draws on the oral history of the suppression of the indigenous Tatar Muslim minority, who returned to the peninsula in the 1990s following independence after years of exile from their homeland.

Much of what we know of life in Crimea since 2014 has come from activists turned citizen journalists. This is one of the reasons the Russian authorities have cracked down so hard on Tatars, characterising them either as political extremists or Islamist terrorists linked to the group Hizb ut-Tahrir.

The testimonies that form the basis of Crimea, 5am were collected by the Crimean Tatar political scientist and activist Lenora Dyulber, who remains in the occupied peninsula under constant risk of arrest from the authorities. These interviews, some over two hours long, were then dramatised by two Ukrainian writers, Anastasiia Kosodii and Natalia Vorozhbyt. The project is backed by the Ukrainian Institute and the Ukrainian Ministry of Foreign Affairs as a way of bringing the situation in Crimea to international attention.

The play, of which an extract is published below, focuses on the domestic lives of the families of the Tatar political prisoners and particularly the women. Kosodii told Index she and her co-author wanted to highlight the specific situation the families of the activists found themselves in after the arrest of their menfolk. In most cases, these were traditional Muslim families: "They often had two or three children, these young women. They had been sheltered by their husbands and didn't have to face reality. Now they had to learn everything from paying the bills to dealing with Russian hostility." All this while continuing to hold their families together.

Since the invasion of February 2022, Kosodii has been dividing her time between Germany and Ukraine, where she is an established playwright and director. Speaking to Index from Berlin, she added: "It was important to give space to these women's experiences, which are often not talked about." She found in the women a common thread of romantic nostalgia about meeting their partner, which contrasted with the brutal reality of life after arrest and separation.

Since the original interviews took place, much has changed in Crimea. It is no longer the case, for instance, that Tatar men are being singled out for arrest. Women too are being rounded up. And the escalation of the conflict has had other horrifying consequences: "The atmosphere is more toxic," said Kosodii. "With the mobilisation, [the Russians] were keen to enlist as many Crimean Tatars as possible to use them as meat on the battlefield."

Readings of the play have taken place in Ukraine itself, as well as around

Europe. One such performance was in January at the Kiln Theatre, Kilburn in London with professional actors working alongside non-professional activists and supporters. The English adaptation was directed by Josephine Burton and produced by Dash Arts. Burton told Index that until the 2022 Russian invasion of Ukraine, Crimea had drifted from international attention. "Helped by a media blackout, we forgot that the peninsula has been occupied by Russians for almost nine years now and its Tatar community oppressed," she said. "Determined to fight this silence, the community has relentlessly documented this oppression – filming and uploading searches, arrests and court cases of its people by the Russian security forces. And for this act, these

citizen journalists have been arrested themselves and given insanely long sentences, some for up to 20 years in penal colonies."

She felt the focus on the families helped bring the struggle of the Tatars to life.

"It builds a beautiful and powerful portrait of a community, ripped apart by this tragedy, but also woven with stories of love and resilience through the prism of the wives left behind. It is this mix of tenderness and humour, alongside the unfathomable darkness, which enables its impact. We the audience become invested in their lives and feel the impact of their tragedy deeply."

Burton and Dash Arts are looking for further opportunities to perform Crimea, 5am in the UK and Europe. Meanwhile,

the Ukrainian team behind Crimea, 5am is developing a documentary based on the play with director Dmytro Kostiumynskyi. This will have to wait, however, until Kostiumynskyi himself returns from the front.

Martin Bright is editor-at-large at Index

From Crimea, 5am

By ANASTASIIA KOSODII and NATALIA VOROZHBYT

DILIARA IBRAHIMOVA: FIFTEEN people entered at once, they showed the warrant straight away, which said... well, namely, that he was facing from 20 years to a life sentence in prison. And so they began searching the living room here, examined our computer top to bottom, then took his phone and afterwards they slowly, step by step, moved to the hall, the kitchen, rummaged through the freezer of all things, the microwave, they got their hands on every mug, every bowl... When asked what on earth it was they were looking for, they said it was about literature, weapons and so on... When they finally reached the bedroom, they turned their attention to the children's backpacks, investigating every page of the record books and the notebooks.

INVESTIGATOR: Aren't the children supposed to be leaving for school? You usually send them to school at this hour, right?

DILIARA IBRAHIMOVA: And it so happened that he looked through her record book and said:

INVESTIGATOR: So what, your daughter is an A-student, isn't she?

Investigator turns to the children.

INVESTIGATOR: What study groups did you attend?

CHILD: Gymnastics.

INVESTIGATOR: Any others? You study Arabic, don't you?

CHILD: Yes.

INVESTIGATOR: Do you like gymnastics?

CHILD 2: I have one Arabic class. The one where we study Sīrah ...

INVESTIGATOR: Could you perhaps tell us more about the difference? Just in case somebody doesn't know what it all means.   ➔

→ CHILD: Well, we study Sīrah, we learn about the different prophets, their deeds, for example, their dominions.

INVESTIGATOR: Who's your favourite prophet?

CHILD 2: My favourite prophet is Suleiman.

INVESTIGATOR: Hm, Suleiman. And why is that so?

CHILD 2: Because he loves animals.

INVESTIGATOR: Loves animals...

CHILD: I like Mohammed, because he was truthful, that's why they called him Al Amin.

INVESTIGATOR: And what kind of animals do you like?

CHILD 2: Tigers.

INVESTIGATOR: Tigers? Is that because they are strong? Or because of their luscious fur?

CHILD: And I like rabbits, they are cute and fluffy.

INVESTIGATOR: They are also very fast runners.

CHILD: Yes, and very high jumpers.

INVESTIGATOR: High jumpers, indeed. Now, do you like school? What's your favourite subject?

CHILD 2: I like all the subjects. I am the best at tables in my class.

INVESTIGATOR: Oh, you are, aren't you?

CHILD 2: Well, we are A-students.

INVESTIGATOR: I see, yeah, I can see that you're A-students, right...

DILIARA IBRAHIMOVA: They went on to empty the bags and scattered the toys around on the floor, and I wondered, "Now, what do you expect to find there? Inside the toys?" And they said:

THEY: What if you hid something inside, who knows, what if you thought we wouldn't check there?

SURIA SHEIKHALIEVA: Well, they didn't make a complete mess, didn't check everything. Just took those books over there and, well, he also had that CD... He had performed Hajj twice, and he kept all the pictures on that CD. Well, there were also these two books, namely, "The History of the Prophets" and "The Meadows of the Righteous," and it was, namely, all about these, they are sort of considered extremist materials and, that said, illegal. Just like that

TYMUR IBRAHIMOV: I need to call my lawyer.

INVESTIGATOR: Now, take it easy, call whoever you want. I couldn't care less.

DILIARA IBRAHIMOVA: And so he called Emil Kurbedinov, who told Tymur:

EMIL KURBEDINOV: If nothing was retrieved, like, if they found nothing, you can sign it without problems.

DILIARA IBRAHIMOVA: There was no real hostility, no, toward the end the investigator himself came up to me and said:

INVESTIGATOR: Go pack him some food and water, sandwiches or whatnot, all the necessary things, comfortable clothes, because he is not coming back soon. No, he is not coming back, mind you, so he'll need some food, water, etc. It's very important.

DILIARA IBRAHIMOVA: I packed him sandwiches, a bottle of water, a change of clothes, even slippers... But they didn't take it, the package, they just left it... Some days later we managed to send it over, after all.

TYMUR IBRAHIMOV: I've been happy with you.

Like, we've lived together for all these years, and I have no bone to pick, no.

DILIARA IBRAHIMOVA: You see, the truth is, we have no idea, if it's the end or just the beginning, or... In such moments one cannot tell for sure, and what is left for a wife? All she wants to hear is her husband's *razlikh*, those crucial words.

MUMINE SALIEVA: It came to me that the only possible way to more or less maintain one's health in those circumstances would be to work out. So I said to him, "Hey, don't forget to exercise." And he said, "Okay." He was about to leave, when I added, "If something was wrong, you know, like, ever, I am very sorry, forgive me," but he replied, "What are you talking about? I am happy with you."

ELZARA SULEIMANOVA: When mother asked to let her say goodbye to her own son, they assured her, "Yes, yes, of course, you'll have time for that," but then, we missed the moment he was gone, had no idea when or where, and one of the officers told me, "They must have already taken him by now, the investigation goes on."

LEMARA MEMEDEMINOVA: The little ones cried their eyes out. But then again, you see, it was the second search, I suppose, they must have expected him to come back... The scene would repeat itself again and again: every time the door opened, they would run to have a look... it lasted several months, that thing with the door... Even when someone came for a visit, like, relatives, I would always tell them to be quiet, "Don't make any noise, otherwise the children will take off running."

ZULFIE SHEIKHALIEVA: He told me he loved me and also ordered me not to cry. [The voice is soft and trembling]. Yeah, he would always bring me dolls, sweets, you know, these very pretty L.O.L. dolls, he would always bring them. He also brought home a cake every Friday, either a raspberry or a caramel one.

ELZARA SULEIMANOVA: Our eldest son remained calm throughout the whole thing. It was only later, after the search, that he seemed, like, hostile, or rather nervous... He later said, "They took him away, and with *babaka* they took away all our joy."

ALL WOMEN TOGETHER, AS IF IT WERE A SPELL: Every burden brings alleviation.

NARIMAN MEMEDEMINOV: They wrenched the door, got inside, threw me on the ground, handcuffed – and that was it. The rest of it went smoothly, nobody raised hell, it was all civilised... Let's say, they were, like, really insistent about the warrant, the search and so on. They spent a lot of time just writing things down, namely, there wasn't much actual searching going on. And at long last they rejoiced, no, that's the wrong word... they triumphed. They found my Ukrainian passport, right here, on the shelf.

SINGER (SURIA): And when they took him away... I... it was as if I knew that he was leaving, but at the same time knew that it all wouldn't last, it would be over and he would be back, yes, so when they asked me to bid him farewell, I refused: "We won't say farewells, you will be back." And when the next morning, I was collecting things, because he left with empty hands, I gave him nothing, they told me, "Get his things! Only necessities!," I refused: "I won't, I won't get him anything, won't, he'll come back, he is about to be back" — and I was so sure, it couldn't be true, no... And when they were walking him, imagine, I didn't cry, I haven't shed a tear, no, only after they drove him away could I break down into tears, because I was attached, I was attached to him that much.

ALL WOMEN TOGETHER, AS IF IT WERE A SPELL: Every burden brings alleviation. ✖

Crimea, 5am tells the story of 10 political prisoners. Read Crimean Tatar Nariman Dzhelal's essay on p.16

52(01):108/111|DOI:10.1177/03064220231165411

LAST WORD

From hijacker to media mogul

SOE MYINT, an activist and journalist, on keeping hope alive in Myanmar

N 1990 THAI International Airways was on route to Yangon when two students hijacked the plane. The hijacking, by Soe Myint and Htin Kyaw Oo, came in the wake of protests over military rule in Myanmar. Using a "bomb" (actually bars of soap with wires attached) they forced the plane to divert to Kolkata and surrendered to the authorities, claiming political asylum. In 1998 Myint and fellow democracy protester Thin Thin Aung founded Mizzima in New Delhi as an exile-based media organisation covering Myanmar. After the political reforms of 2012, Mizzima returned to Myanmar as a local media entity. The military under General Min Aung Hlaing once again took control in a coup in 2021.

INDEX What are your thoughts two years on from the military coup?

SOE MYINT I am amazed by the resilience of the Myanmar people to military rule and attempts by the junta to deny their basic rights. Especially the younger generations, who have taken it upon themselves, at the cost of much hardship and risk to their lives, to lead the fight against the junta. We have witnessed

a coming together of various forces in opposition to the junta. And for the first time in the history of Myanmar we are seeing collaboration between large swathes of the Burman population and ethnic minorities. This collaboration and common vision of federalism is an opportunity for Myanmar's future which cannot be lost.

INDEX What has been the reaction to the extension of the state of emergency until August?

SOE MYINT We always knew this was one possibility. And it signifies the weakness of the junta. At the time of the announcement Min Aung Hlaing acknowledged that more than a third of townships were not under its control. This was assuredly an underestimation, as the townships declared by the junta to be under martial law as of February 2023 are actually townships without any military control. The extension of the state of emergency has done little other than further steel the resolve of Myanmar's pro-democracy forces.

INDEX Do you think elections will be free and fair when they happen?

SOE MYINT There is no chance of elections being free and fair. A component of Min Aung Hlaing's coup was to set the stage to reorient the country's politics, which the military felt was getting out of its control... It is also a necessity for a pro-military 'party' to emerge victorious from any 'elections' as that would serve to protect Min Aung Hlaing and other members of the security sector from facing possible measures of accountability.

INDEX What is the outlook for independent media such as Mizzima?

SOE MYINT The junta is facing severe challenges to its rule. By some estimates around half the country is now outside its jurisdiction. In trying to justify its

PICTURED: Soe Myint, who runs Myanmar's leading independent media house Mizzima

rule over the remainder of the country, it is essential that it controls the narrative. This narrative, which paints opposition forces as terrorists as well as claiming erroneous military gains in the conflict, is seriously challenged by independent media reports. It is no coincidence that Myanmar's independent media, such as Mizzima, were meant to cease to exist with the 1 February 2021 coup. Mizzima was banned from officially operating inside Myanmar and was again forced to adopt a mode of operations reliant on an exile presence to support clandestine activities inside Myanmar.

Our audience numbers since the coup have realised dramatic increases as the people of Myanmar thirst for reliable and accurate information. Mizzima's main Facebook page now has almost 22 million followers. According to an independent national media survey carried out in September-October 2022, Mizzima was the most popular source for news in Myanmar in 2022.

INDEX If you were detained and could take one book to jail with you, what would it be?

SOE MYINT I wish I could take a few books but Nelson Mandela's Long Walk to Freedom would be one of them.

INDEX What piece of art has affected you the most?

SOE MYINT Street magicians in Myanmar.

INDEX What news headline would you most like to read?

SOE MYINT Myanmar military leader Min Aung Hlaing flees to Russia and seeks asylum. ✖

52(01):112/112|DOI:10.1177/03064220231165412